The Failure of Modern Architecture

Brent C. Brolin

VNR VAN NOSTRAND REINHOLD COMPANY
New York   Cincinnati   Toronto   London   Melbourne

**This book is dedicated to my parents,
Ed and Netta Brolin.**

Copyright © 1976 by Brent Brolin
Library of Congress Catalog Card Number: 75-23922
ISBN 0-442-21070-1 (cloth)

Printed in the United States of America.
Designed by Loudan Enterprises
All photographs are by the author unless otherwise credited.

Published in 1976 by Van Nostrand Reinhold Compny
A Division of Litton Educational Publishing, Inc.
450 West 33rd Street
New York, NY 10001

Van Nostrand Reinhold Limited
1410 Birchmount Road
Scarborough, Ontario M1P 2E7, Canada

Van Nostrand Reinhold Australia Pty. Ltd.
17 Queen Street
Mitcham, Victoria 3132, Australia

Van Nostrand Reinhold Company Ltd.
Molly Millars Lane
Wokingham, Berkshire, England

16 15 14 13 12 11 10 9 8 7 6 5 4 3 2 1

Library of Congress Cataloging in Publication Data

Brolin, Brent C.
    The failure of modern architecture.

    Bibliography: p.
    Includes index.
    1. Architecture, Modern—20th century. 2. Architec-
ture—Psychological aspects. 3. Architecture and
society. I. Title.
NA680.B76   724.9   75-23922
ISBN 0-442-21070-1

In addition to the credits given in the captions themselves, the
author and publisher gratefully acknowledge permission to
reproduce Fig. 2-60. Reprinted from *The Bauhaus* by Hans
Wingler by permission of the M.I.T. Press, Cambridge,
Massachusetts. © 1969 M.I.T. Press.

Acknowledgments

I would like to thank Eva Zeisel for planting the seeds many years ago that grew into these thoughts and for helping periodically, with generosity and humor as well as insight, in their cultivation.

My appreciation also to the New York Public Library and the Avery Architectural Library of Columbia University for concentrating so much valuable information and for making it so readily available, for the courtesy of their staffs and for their generosity in permitting the use of some of the illustrations in this book.

Thanks also to Ann, Hans, Toby and Peter for taking time at various stages to read and criticize the manuscript, and to John Zeisel, my partner on several projects that appear as examples in this book.

Contents

[The] protagonists of One World have staked their hopes on
convincing people of every corner of the earth that all the
differences between East and West, black and white, Christian
and Mohammedan, are superficial and that all mankind is really
like-minded.... It sometimes seems as if the tender-minded
could not base a doctrine of good will upon anything less than
a world of peoples, each of which is a print from the same
negative. But to demand such uniformity as a condition of
respecting another nation is as neurotic as to demand it of one's
wife or one's children. The tough-minded are content that
differences should exist...

—Ruth Benedict, *The Chrysanthemum and the Sword*

Foreword

For over half a century modern architecture has been guided by nineteenth-century principles. It is difficult to look beyond the modern ideology because we have been educated to consider it as the only acceptable set of architectural rules. It has become a sanctified body of knowledge, assumed to operate always, and seldom if ever questioned. So ingrained have its tenets become that we resort to them as a reflex action. Thinking in any other terms is almost impossible. And yet these principles no longer apply to the world in which the architect now works.

This book was conceived some eight years ago when, upon leaving the rarefied atmosphere of architecture school, I contacted the real world and tried to put into practice what I had been taught.

I soon realized that the rules taught in school were irrelevant and even destructive when put into practice, and I began asking myself how these particular rules came to be the only ones taught in architecture school. I hope that this book will help to free the layman and the student of architecture from the sacred cow of modern architectural ideology by giving them some perspective on how it was formed. It is hoped that by realizing how indirect and irrelevant the cultural inspirations for these ideas were, they will be able to see more clearly why the tenets are no longer acceptable rationalizations for twentieth-century architecture.

—Brent C. Brolin

I.

Introduction

Modern architects face problems today that they are ill-equipped to handle:

—After fifty years of indoctrination the majority of the public remains indifferent or hostile to the modern aesthetic. The predicted universal acceptance of modern architecture has never come to pass.

—Evidence shows that throughout the world modern architectural and planning ideas have failed wherever the architect disregards the social and aesthetic values of the user. Some signs of this condition include:

A growing reaction against modern buildings in traditional contexts that try to be "different" rather than fit in. And a new disposition of non-Western cultures, which formerly accepted modern architecture because of a sense of cultural inferiority, to try to recapture their own traditional visual and social values.

The disillusionment with modern architecture came about because architects imposed their values on a public that did not share them.

VISUAL IMPOSITIONS

The proponents of modern international architecture say that its universal form-language is the logical outcome of a rational approach to design with new materials and techniques. The bewildered onlooker is told that these new forms, devoid of heritage, are "functional" or "economical" or "dictated by new materials and techniques," but these are simply rationalizations for style preferences. There is no practical inevitability to modern forms.

Modern architecture intentionally defies its older neighbors rather than standing beside them in peace. It tries to shock rather than sympathize.

While architects look upon the new architecture with pride, laymen eye it warily. At the Osaka World's Fair, a "city of tomorrow" was shown embodying the most advanced concepts of modern architecture and planning. Unaware of these advantages, the tour guides miscalled the exhibit the "city of sorrows."

Yale University Art Gallery. The old art gallery is at the right and an addition, by Louis Kahn in 1953, at the left.

Old and new in Sanaa, Yemen.

Old and new in Venice, Italy.

The specter of anonymity haunts modern housing like this building in Washington, D.C.

Even prize-winning examples of modern architecture are seldom popularly embraced, as for example the Boston City Hall shown here. Public apathy is largely due to the fact that the majority of people are disturbed by the sterile appearance of modern buildings and are not interested in the intellectual ideas that buildings represent.

Office buildings on Avenue of the Americas in New York City. Ca. nineteen-sixties.

Boston City Hall; Kallman, McKinnel and Knowles, architects; 1969. In the February 1973 issue of *Architecture Plus* Ellen Perry Berkeley wrote: "It is not surprising, therefore, that many Bostonians, unfamiliar with the articles of faith of modern architecture, should consider this building a grandiose, extravagant and ultimately distasteful work."

The anonymity of modern housing offers a harsh contrast to the human scale of most suburban developments. Shown above: Kips Bay Apartments in New York City; I. M. Pei, architect; 1965. Below: Alexandria, Virginia, suburb.

Wherever Western civilization has penetrated, impersonal forms intrude upon the traditional profiles of cities, towns and villages. Whereas even as recently as ten years ago the traveler found unexpected delights, he is now faced with stultifying predictability in the architecture. He flies from New York to Beirut—or Kabul or Delhi or Hong Kong—and hardly knows that he has changed countries.

In spite of the generally held belief fostered by modern architecture that technological societies share a common cultural denominator, each culture retains strong links to its own past. One way of expressing this connection is through visual traditions, but these have been intentionally excluded from modern cities throughout the world. The spiritual loss is real and people of all cultures sense it.

Modern housing in Taipei, Taiwan. (Courtesy of the Chinese Information Service)

Modern housing in Teheran, Iran.

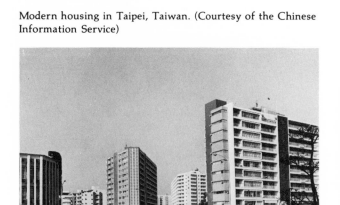

Modern housing in Kabul, Afghanistan.

SOCIAL IMPOSITIONS

The visual preferences of the modern movement were accompanied by implicit assumptions about how people live or how they should live—assumptions defined by the architect's personal values and built into each design by his placement of doors, windows and walls. The architect assumed that the world shared these values or would soon accept them, but by and large they have been rejected.

Few laymen or professionals see any alternatives to the prevalent sterile, anonymous architecture and the ideology that defends it. The most resigned layman assumes this architecture's naked forms come from economic necessity; the most enthusiastic sees it as a symbol of prosperity and modernity. In either case, there has never seemed to be a choice about it because modern architecture has never been presented as a "style"; it has been considered a movement of "truths" for so long that we are unable to think of it as a set of arbitrary, systematized aesthetic choices. By now, it has become an ideological prison that traps professional and nonprofessional alike as soon as they are initiated into its rules.

However, as the following chapters will indicate, there are alternatives, and if architects and interested laymen become aware of them, they will see that the austere forms of modern architecture are not inviolate, that there is no modern morality to wrestle with since the "truths" of the movement have no moral basis.

To recognize this, first we have to unlearn what modern architects have been preaching to us for the past half century. To help in this process the following chapters describe the various cultural currents of the nineteenth century that together formed the basis of modern architecture's stylistic rationalizations that now seem so difficult to question. The practical application of these visual and social premises is examined in isolated examples and in two larger case studies. And, finally, in the last chapter the boundaries of the architect's influence and the extent of his responsibilities in our multicultural world are considered.

II.

The Cultural Roots of Modern Architecture

In the early twentieth century an architectural revolution took place. All traditional styles were declared null and void—to the point where putting ornament on a building was regarded as a criminal act. Instead of admiring Michelangelo or the Gothic cathedrals, as before, architects now looked to airplanes, factories and industrial machines for inspiration. This aesthetic revolution took place for two main reasons:

1. Technological progress offered new building materials. In the nineteenth century, when glass, iron, steel and reinforced concrete were first being explored, they had not been considered "architectural" materials. Architectural design was based on historical precedents and, of course, there were no precedents for these new materials. The modernists felt that the new materials should be exploited to help find solutions to modern architectural and urban problems. Breaking with architectural tradition facilitated the uninhibited exploration of the new materials and methods.

2. The flowering of capitalism in the nineteenth century created a growing wealthy middle class. Because inexpensive manufactured goods were now available, the middle class could buy things that previously only the rich could afford. The variety and inventiveness of ornamental styles were staggering in the nineteenth century, and sophisticated artists and critics became disturbed

by people's overindulgence and lack of what they considered discriminating taste.

Artists, searching for ways to control the proliferation of styles spurred by technical capability and market demand, established rules to define which kinds of ornament were good and which were bad, and which forms were appropriate to a function and which were not. The guide lines did not help: the middle classes would not be dissuaded from or directed in their lust for sumptuous ornament.

The profusion of ornament was a crucial factor in the estrangement of the architect from society that culminated in the modern architectural revolution. This revolution solved the problem of middle-class taste for the architect by eliminating it as an alternative. Demanding that all traditions be abandoned, modernists forged a completely new aesthetic. The question was, would the people follow? They did not. And this break with popular taste was the beginning of the elitist modern architecture of today.

Rules of compelling moral force had to be established to make the break with tradition comprehensible and acceptable to the public. To help legitimize the new architecture leaders of the movement, such as Walter Gropius, described their creations as the "inevitable result" of a logical process of design. Modern architecture looked the way it did simply because architects obeyed certain demands: *honesty* of materials; *honesty* of structure; *honesty* in that the function of a building is reflected in its forms; an apparent evolutionary bias favoring simplicity; *honesty* that reflects the true spirit of the times in its architecture rather than reflecting elements of the past; and the demand that architects be *true* to themselves. The morality of modern architecture had great advantages: styles can change, but there is no alternative to Truth.

Modern architecture's obvious sources of visual inspiration are the basically simple, "clean" and coldly precise qualities that were first appreciated in the tools of modern times: airplanes, ships, heavy and light machinery and industrial buildings. These became the basis of modern architecture's antitraditional iconography.

Realizing intuitively how unpopular their position was, modernists were careful not to let their aesthetic choices stand only on visual merits. They never said that people would accept modern architecture because it was more beautiful than traditional architecture. Although they theorized about a *visual* art, they rationalized their visual choices in exclusively *moral* terms.

The honesties and truths with which modernists still defend their architecture have no direct bearing on what makes buildings beautiful or cities livable. The truths of the new architecture were inferred from traditions of Protestantism, nineteenth-century capitalism and from the rising influence of science and technology in everyday life. As used by architects, the potency of these truths lay precisely in the fact that they harked back to some of the basic premises of Western industrial society.

The transference of ideas from these diverse sources to architecture was primarily a matter of poetic associations. When an ideal or a practice is successful in one field of endeavor, it is often irrationally adopted by another. The aura of success or novelty carries over from the original context to the new situation and provides approval by association. For example, advertisers, who often rely on this sort of poetic association, today apply the shapes of astronauts' paraphernalia to everything from whiskey bottles to stereo sets.

Thus modern architects, using poetic associations devoid of any rational basis, relied on the moral weight of culturally accepted premises to enforce essentially unpopular aesthetic choices. The ideas grafted onto architecture came from a number of different influences:

1. From capitalism—that system wherein all energies are aimed at increasing efficiency, at getting the most return for the least investment—modernists acquired the intellectual and emotional bias for a practical, functional approach to design. This approach worked toward the exclusion of all elements, such as ornament, that served no demonstrably practical purpose, and the rejection of visual complexity in favor of simple forms that, it was felt, would better serve the simple, basic needs of life.

A stereo radio and tape player in the form of a space helmet, from the late nineteen-sixties.

2. From the Protestant ethic, which attributed moral values to nonmoral activities such as "hard work," came the tendency to attribute moral values to nonmoral, specifically aesthetic, choices. Truth and Beauty have often been linked, but the modern movement offered one of the more precise formulas for joining the two: it was honest and beautiful to show materials in their natural state—dishonest and ugly to disguise them; honest to express the structure of a building on the exterior—dishonest to disguise it; honest to express the function of a building—dishonest to obscure it. It was felt that the application of these and other moral imperatives represented direct, positive, steps toward curing urban problems.

3. A self-righteousness comparable only to that of the nineteenth-century Christian missionary led architects to assume that their own attitudes and values were proper for all others in the modern world, regardless of class, race or cultural differences.

4. Deified Reason, science and the revered engineer supplanted tradition as the source of truth. This facilitated the fall of traditional architectural styles and the rise of the modern aesthetic. Factory architecture and machines—the engineer's creations—were venerated not only for their clean look, but also because they embodied the epitome of functional design: they were made expressly for *one* purpose.

5. Technological and scientific successes encouraged the worship of change. It followed from a belief in the inevitable improvement of life through technology that social and aesthetic traditions were irrelevant.

6. The erroneous popular understanding of Darwin's theory of evolution led people to believe that the physical environment was the critical factor in social behavior and that by changing an unsatisfactory environment, social harmony could be restored. This misunderstanding also lent the apparent support of natural law to the idea that non-practical elements such as ornament should be eliminated just as a species' unused organs atrophy.

UTILITY AND ORNAMENT: THE EFFECTS OF CAPITALISM AND THE PROTESTANT ETHIC

The most publicized attribute of modern architecture has been its "functionalism," the quality of fulfilling a purpose directly, without any wasted effort. Functionalism was a particularly successful rallying cry against the eclectic architecture of the nineteenth century that included all kinds of familiar and exotic "impractical" decoration.

Simplicity of architectural form went hand in hand with functionalism. Simplifying a building without impairing its ability to serve its purpose meant getting rid of nonessentials; the building's "functional" quality was thus enhanced.

The nineteenth-century concept of economizing action was one of the main sources of functional architecture and its companion, simple architectural forms. In his book, *Primitive, Archaic and Modern Economies*, the economic historian Karl Polanyi defines economizing action as the attempt to eliminate everything that is not useful or necessary in practical terms. Although the concept originated earlier, the economizing, utilitarian ideal had permeated every aspect of life by the nineteenth century because it was essential both to capitalism and the Protestant work ethic.

The role of economizing action in capitalism is obvious: economy means efficiency, which means more profits, which means more capital to reinvest. As capitalism blossomed, the concept of economizing action became so much a part of life that it was assumed man had always been driven by the need to work efficiently. Man's first creations were believed to have been simple, unadorned tools and his "natural" first choices had presumably been directed to satisfying utilitarian rather than spiritual or aesthetic needs. It was assumed that except for decadent societies, man's basic drive has always been, and was still, the elimination of all "unproductive" work.

The popular acceptance of economizing action and its implicit practical bias can be seen in the way the meaning of the word "utilitarian" changed as the importance of capitalism grew during the first half of the nineteenth century.

In 1789, Jeremy Bentham had expounded a philosophy founded on the principle of "utility" in *An Introduction to the Principles of Morals and Legislation.* He gave the concept a broad range of meanings, encompassing anything that supplied "the greatest good to the greatest number of people."

The 11ᵗʰ commandment: Thou shalt make a profit.

Protestantism and capitalism have been mutually supportive since shortly after the Reformation, when it was recognized that the Protestant work ethic was a crucial factor in the development of a thriving mercantile empire. Both influences shaped the rules of modern architecture. (Courtesy of *Forbes* Magazine)

It could apply equally to an impractical statue in the park, because it was a source of civic pride and inspired good citizenship, or to the practical machines of industry that made life's necessities and luxuries available to larger numbers of people.

By the middle of the nineteenth century, however, Bentham's broadly defined ideal of utility had become hopelessly distorted. It was so intertwined with industry's demand for economy and the preachings against temptations of sensual pleasure, growing out of the residue of Puritanism, that it eventually became associated with, among other things, lack of ornament and simplicity. John Stuart Mill, a follower of Bentham and a proponent of utilitarianism, was frustrated by this crucial misunderstanding and attacked the public's perversion of Bentham's principle in his essay, *Utilitarianism,* published in 1863:

> Those who know anything about the matter are aware that every writer, from Epicurus to Bentham, who maintained the theory of utility, meant by it, not something to be contradistinguished from pleasure, but pleasure itself, together with exemption from pain; and instead of opposing the useful to the agreeable or the ornamental, have always declared that the useful means these, among other things. Yet the common herd ... are perpetually falling into this shallow mistake. *Having caught up the word utilitarian while knowing nothing whatever about it but its sound, they habitually express by it the rejection, or the neglect of pleasure in some of its forms: of beauty, or ornament, or of amusement.* Nor is the term thus ignorantly misapplied solely in disparagement, but occasionally in compliment, *as though it implied a superiority to frivolity and the mere pleasures of the moment.*[1]
> [Author's italics]

This popular misconception of utilitarianism, tempered by the economic necessities of capitalism and the Puritanical compulsion for work rather than play, held the seeds of the moral and practical biases that would guide modern design. Sixty years later the visual character of modern architecture showed their influence: restraint rather than indulgence; simplicity rather than complexity.

Economizing action was also essential to the Protestant work ethic. The goals of a simple life and abstention from worldly excesses had been the major thrust of Protestantism since Luther's break with the Roman Church.

Self-denial was one sign of devotion to God. Yet at the same time that the faithful Lutheran, Calvinist or Puritan was not supposed to surrender to worldly pleasures, he was expected to be a good businessman and to be aggressive in this world. It was as sinful to be concerned only with the spiritual world as it was to be devoted exclusively to the material world. The Protestant capacity for hard work proved legendary. As John Calvin, felled by fever, stones, gout and asthma, lay near death, he continued to drive himself. When his friends urged him to slow down, he is said to have replied: "Would you that the Lord should find me idle when He comes?"

Although Puritanism was ultimately banished to the New World, the work ethic of this rightwing Protestantism left an indelible impression on Europe. In England, the most telling influence, in terms of our discussion, was the Puritan insistence on the social importance of work and a view of life shaped by the principle of utility. If not a help toward salvation, success in worldly affairs gained through hard work was at least a sign that you were in God's grace. Therefore, as already mentioned, it was as important to pursue one's earthly calling with hard work, and by one's successes appear to have obtained God's favor, as it was to pursue one's spiritual calling by prayer. Laziness had been condemned for a number of practical and religious reasons in the seventeenth century. It was recognized that a lazy work force had serious consequences for a country's economy; without productive workers England could not compete in world trade. From a spiritual standpoint, idleness was abhorred because it allowed time to contemplate the Devil.

The modernists' point of view that decoration serves no purpose and is therefore somehow immoral is totally in sympathy with Protestant ideals. However, the goals of simplicity and utility that supposedly governed the economic and private life of the eighteenth-century merchant seem irreconcilable with the fact that most items of daily life—from snuff boxes to kitchen utensils—were, if at all possible, richly ornamented.

An ornamental, utilitarian object in daily use in the eighteenth century: an iron trivet.

Although modernists would regard this ornamentation as neither economical nor utilitarian, our ancestors apparently had no such narrow definition. They considered utility a necessary condition for beauty, but this in no way precluded ornament. The noted eighteenth-century English engraver, William Hogarth, in his *Analysis of Beauty* wrote that his appreciation of a sailing ship came from knowing that each part was carefully fitted to its purpose. From the modern viewpoint, forgetting that Hogarth probably never saw a sailing ship, even a warship, that was not ornamented in some fashion, we might easily misunderstand this statement. Utility was certainly one of the components of beauty, but the definition of utility seldom went beyond the simple demand that neither construction nor decoration should impede the intended use.

The rise of the bourgeoisie as tastemakers caused a gradual change in the balance struck between ornament and utility. Members of the aristocracy had traditionally determined the constituents of beauty. They were the only ones wealthy enough to pay for, or powerful enough to command, works of art. But with the eighteenth and nineteenth centuries a hard-working middle class had grown up that owed its new economic power largely to its utilitarian ethic. As the means of acquiring worldly goods came within the reach of more and more people, the fears of worldly temptation seemed to diminish. Social standing now hinged more on financial success, so that wealth and the things it could buy became a primary indicator of status. The industrial revolution had created a middle class whose wealth allowed it to establish its own definition of beauty and good taste and whose industrial techniques had made its taste in decorated goods accessible to almost all people.

Even the most functional sailing ships had a full complement of decoration, right down to the garlanded cannon portals. This is the warship *Paris*, executed in 1669 by Pierre Puget. (Courtesy of General Research and Humanities Division, The New York Public Library. Astor, Lenox and Tilden Foundations)

For example, before industrialization only the wealthy could afford finely decorated fabrics, while others had to be satisfied with simple home-spun goods. But power looms and large-scale textile printing made it possible for an increasing number of people to afford relatively inexpensive printed imitations of the hand-painted fabrics the wealthy were wearing.

Mass production allowed inexpensive imitations of goods so costly that only the wealthy could afford them before: "This lively-looking steam print, so well executed that it reminds us of the early days of calico-printing, when such a pattern would have been finished by the camel's-hair brush, a slow process of production which contrasts strongly with the rapidity of the present day...." (Excerpt and illustration from *Journal of Design and Manufactures*, No. 14, 1850; Courtesy of the Avery Architecture Library, Columbia University)

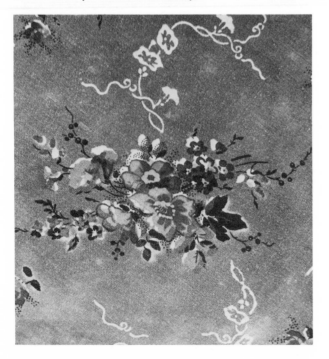

By the late eighteenth century machines had been introduced into ceramic manufacturing and for the first time pottery mimicking the fine porcelain of the nobility was also available on a large scale.

The nouveaux riches clamored for more and more elaborate ornament—the most tangible sign of richness—and the artistic and intellectual elite, appalled at their overindulgences, turned away in disgust. They found moral justification for their repugnance in the very utility-oriented bias of Protestantism that had helped create the new middle classes. The new fashion of encrusting objects with ornament was declared nonfunctional; it was said to interfere with the object's utility.

Yet, at this stage, critics were careful not to condemn all ornament—only inappropriate ornament. In establishing which ornament was appropriate and which was not, they fell back on the concept of utility as it had been understood by Hogarth in the previous century. Ornament was in bad taste if it interfered with utility and so detracted from beauty; but interfering with utility was interpreted differently in the nineteenth century than it would be now.

Given our modern definition of "functional," which equates fitness of purpose with the elimination of ornament, nineteenth-century discussions of appropriate and inappropriate ornament are almost incomprehensible. Consider this critique of ornamented candlesticks from the *Journal of Design and Manufactures* in 1850: "In the more ornamental one [candlestick], the decoration is properly controlled and made strictly subordinate to utility, as it ought to be." Evidently, the quantity of ornament does not determine utility, since the more heavily ornamented candlestick, shown in the first photograph is judged to be better suited for its purpose.

The butter dish embellished with a Greek frieze and a pitcher wrapped in a grapevine motif shown in the next two illustrations occasioned a similar discussion. The pitcher is considered appropriately decorated, while the butter dish is not. From the modern viewpoint it is difficult to understand the rationale behind this critique, but "appropriateness" in this case would seem to be measured by at least two criteria:

1. The graphic character of the motif and the object it adorns should be similar—either curvilinear or angular—and:

2. The associations that the ornament brings to mind should be connected to the use of the object: grape vines are proper for a pitcher that might serve wine, but the Panathenaic procession, topped with a sphinx, has nothing to do with serving butter.

Different principles of decoration were formulated at different times. The English Arts and Crafts Movement, which began in the eighteen-seventies, was led by artists and social critics such as William Morris and Dante Gabriel Rossetti. Directed against the social and aesthetic evils of industrialism, it promoted a revival of medieval design as a way of rejuvenating the English decorative arts and handicrafts. In an effort to define the rules for decoration, Walter Crane, a follower of William Morris, declared a functional criterion for determining its appropriateness. He argued that in the past ornament had been derived from structural necessities—the gothic gargoyle first as a drain spout and second as an ornamental element—and it was appropriate that such utility should continue to determine decoration.

In describing functional ornament from the past, the nineteenth-century art critic John Ruskin cited the Gothic pinnacle in *The Seven Lamps of Architecture*. He saw it as having been a structural member that then became a decorative element. Ornament and business, he felt, should not be mixed, and he complained about the ornamentation of shop fronts, railroad stations and other places or objects whose conditions of use did not encourage the leisurely contemplation of beauty.

English candlesticks, 1850. Although more ornamental, the candlestick on left, is felt to be more functional because its ornament is "strictly subordinate to use." (Courtesy of the Avery Architecture Library, Columbia University)

English ware, 1850. The butter dish in the illustration left is felt to have inappropriate decoration, whereas the pitcher in the illustration right has decoration that is appropriate to its function. (Courtesy of the Avery Architecture Library, Columbia University)

Curiously the illusion of function was as acceptable as the fact. For example, taste-makers such as Charles Eastlake felt that proper carpet or wall decoration should be abstract rather than realistic. Although this obviously had no practical bearing on the use of a floor or wall, it was felt that the illusion of flatness provided by non-realistic decoration was more honest because it did not contradict the flatness or solidity of the surface.

It must be reemphasized that such rules were not promulgated in a vacuum, but came about as reactions to popular taste, which, at that time, actually preferred realism to abstraction.

As we have mentioned, although the rules for judging ornamentation varied, the ornament was not, in itself, considered useless or nonfunctional. It was applied without qualms to all manufactured goods from kitchen utensils to heavy machinery.

St. Joseph's Roman Catholic Church in New York City, 1833. Some felt that ornament was good if it derived its form from honest structural necessities. This gave rise to some inconsistencies. The details of the Doric order evolved when temples were constructed in wood; later, in Classical Greece, the same forms were translated into marble and became purely decorative. In the nineteenth century they were retranslated into wood, as shown here, but without any of the original structural meaning.

The ideal of suitable or appropriate ornament persisted for a time among intellectuals, and there were even calls for the development of a practical science of ornament that would investigate the phenomena of nature to see how better to ornament man-made products. But this ideal was never realized. Instead the decorative excesses resulting from the middle classes' insatiable demand finally so overwhelmed sophisticated observers that the only possible cure seemed to be a violent reaction in favor of simplicity, which would be a vital component of the coming modernism.

The Great Exhibition of 1851 in London was the first of the large international exhibits. Joseph Paxton's Crystal Palace held bay after bay of practical and pleasurable ornate objects, and some participants indicated that the huge quantities of heavily ornamented, mass-produced goods had taken their visual toll. In a special supplement to the official report of the 1851 Exhibition, Richard Redgrave, a patrician painter and inspector-general of the Science and Art department of the South Kensington Museum, spoke of excess ornament "...which is apt to sicken us of decoration, and leads us to admire those objects of absolute utility where use is so paramount that ornament is repudiated, and, fitness of purpose being the end sought, a noble simplicity is the result." Here then, seventy years before the flowering of the modern movement, are the functional justifications for modern architecture's simplicity and the moral tone that was used to rationalize them. It is the foreshadowing moral cast of Redgrave's remarks that is particularly interesting: the lack of decoration is uplifting and the presence of decoration, therefore, degrading. Fifty years later, the Viennese architect Adolph Loos would initiate the modern attack on ornament with stunningly similar logic as he declared in his discourse *Ornament and Crime* that "the evolution of culture marches with the elimination of ornament from useful objects."[2]

The use of ornament also began to suffer because the ornament itself—even if well designed—was commonly of poor quality. Often a critic's displeasure was based on the fact that the ornament was used to cover shoddy and even dangerous workmanship.

A patent sugar cane crushing mill by Robinsons & Russell in England, 1851. Simple geometric machine forms offered visual relief for the sophisticated viewer who felt that the majority of mass-produced ornaments were in bad taste. (Courtesy of the Avery Architecture Library, Columbia University)

Three examples of the ornament explosion taken from the catalogue of the Great Exhibition in London, 1851: a ceiling ventilator, an inkstand and a candelabrum. (Courtesy of the Avery Architecture Library, Columbia University)

Even those who felt ornament was a vital part of design, such as the champion of architectural ornament, John Ruskin, had doubts about its validity if it was to be mass-produced so crudely. In *The Seven Lamps of Architecture*, he depicted machine-made ornament as one of the three cardinal sins of architecture: it was artistically inferior to handmade ornament and, worse, was a dishonest imitation. He went so far as to hint that the bare bones of the building were preferable to improper ornament—a strikingly modern idea for this mid-nineteenth-century romantic.

The universally mass-produced architectural ornamentation in Ruskin's time forced him grudgingly to admit that engineering works, such as railroad stations—which were not even legitimate architecture in his eyes—had their own potential for dignity if they were left undecorated: "You would not put rings on the fingers of a smithy at his anvil." It was a short step from this admission to the modern architect's idealization of simple, undecorated industrial forms as a defense against the taste of the middle classes.

Gable Ornaments, Adjustable.

Block Pattern No. 14426.

Block Pattern extends 5 feet down the gable, furnished in either one-half or one-third pitch. These ornaments are neat and attractive designs, low in price, and are so constructed any carpenter can regulate to fit any pitch. Gable ornaments add ten times their cost to the appearance of any home.

No. 14426. Block pattern. Price, each........**$2.00**

When ordering state what pitch is wanted.

Low cost, and often low-quality, mass-produced architectural ornament was available to all. These gable ornaments could be purchased from Sears Roebuck circa 1898.

King's Cross Station in London by Lewis Cubitt, 1851-52. Although engineering works were not considered works of art, their stark beauty became more and more appealing to critics like John Ruskin as the quality of decoration declined. (Courtesy of the Avery Architecture Library, Columbia University)

Anti-Ornament

Modernists were enchanted by the new forms and possibilities of the mechanical age. Armed with the Protestant/capitalist bias, which created a moral climate sympathetic to their beloved ideal of simplicity, they used the rejection of ornament as the main weapon in their assault on traditional architecture. After Adolph Loos's equation of ornament with crime in 1908, all major figures in the modern movement stood squarely against ornament as it was traditionally known in architecture. Since all traditions rely in some way on ornament, architecture without ornament meant architecture that did not rely on tradition. Ornamentation on houses, utensils and ritual objects is part of daily life in most cultures, but to modernists it was a sign of decadence. Even within the Greco-Roman tradition the least ornamented architectural order, the Doric order, was singled out for praise above all others by Le Corbusier, the foremost proponent of pure, clean modernism and the single most influential theoretician and practitioner of the movement.

For the first time in history traditional ornament was formally excluded from an architectural philosophy. Whereas Giorgio Vasari, the Renaissance artist and historian, typified the pre-twentieth-century view when he matter-of-factly included ornament while discussing the principles of villa planning, modern architects consciously disdained traditional small-scale ornamental details in favor of bold, if often scaleless expanses: "...we must...transfer questions of taste out of the field of petty mouldings, fiddling capitals and insignificant porticos," wrote the Italian Futurist architect Sant' Elia in 1914, "into the vaster field of the grouping of masses on the grandest scale..."[3]

The visual intricacy of traditional buildings meant that as you approached them, different layers of ornament, at smaller and smaller scales, were revealed. Since something new was being offered, the eye was always entertained and interested. With stripped modern architecture, the inquisitive eye is seldom rewarded. Consider the two buildings in the four accompanying illustrations.

Le Corbusier approved of the Doric order because of its austerity and disapproved of the more flamboyant Corinthian, claiming that there was a moral difference between the discipline of the Doric and the indulgence of the Corinthian. (Courtesy of the Avery Architecture Library, Columbia University)

From a distance the older building has a complicated silhouette and rich surface texture, neither of which is easy to discern. Coming closer, the eye picks out more details of the ornamented silhouette and begins to see specific elements in what were only general textures previously. Then, when one is quite close, one sees variations in materials, textures and even different window details.

When the modern style abandoned the ornament and small-scale details of traditional buildings, there was often little left to hold one's visual interest beyond the basic shape and materials, which are almost always evident from a distance. As exemplified by the building on the left, the traditionally decorated building normally has a much greater range of details to hold one's visual interest. The buildings are viewed together first from a distance, then head-on and then separately.

The modern building next to it is understood at one glance from a distance. It is a hard-edged box made of horizontal bands of glass, steel and brick. If we know something about modern architectural detailing, we may enjoy the subtleties of steel window frames as we approach, but this building differs from the older one in that its windows are all alike. If you've seen one, you've seen them all. The consequences of instant comprehensibility from a distance and lack of close-up variety is that there is no incentive to keep looking—and most people do not.

Fascination with speed encouraged the modern tendency to omit small, human-scaled details. Cities were panoramas to be seen from speeding cars on sweeping highways or, still more extreme, from the air. Architects saw no need for intricate details on which the eye could linger when the giant skyscrapers were only to be background elements reflecting the "blue glory of the sky," as Le Corbusier put it. Urban conceptions were on an intimidating scale—grander than human.

Modern architecture did eventually develop its own simplified versions of ornament—"structural ornament" or "the building as ornament"—but detailed ornamentation, at scales that could be appreciated at different distances, is almost non-existent. Paul Rudolf's interior for the Art and Architecture building at Yale, illustrated here, is a novel exception, both in the use of applied ornament and nonabstract ornament. Yet the architect successfully avoided the trauma of ornamenting the interior himself by borrowing surplus plaster casts from the Yale Art Gallery.

Structure as ornament: above, CBS Building in New York City; Eero Saarinen; 1964—and below, Government Center Garage in Boston; Samuel Glaser & Partners and Kallman McKinnel; 1970. Although modernists frown upon the word "ornament" they often use structural elements in ornamental ways as shown here, where the structure becomes a scaleless ornamental screen.

Traditional ornament versus the modern building as ornament.
The traditional building is the U.S. Customs House; Cass
Gilbert, architect, and Daniel Chester French, sculptor; 1907.

This kind of applied ornament, in the form of leftover plaster
casts, which decorates the interior of the Art and Architecture
Building at Yale University is rare in modern architecture.
(Paul Rudolf, architect; 1963)

Functionalism and Beauty

Although "functionalism" has many shades of meaning, functional architecture implies buildings that serve their purpose efficiently and without any unnecessary elements.

To the modernists, beauty depended to a large degree on the real or imagined attribute of functionalism, to the extent that the Russian Constructivist Vladimir Tatlin could proclaim the aesthetic superiority of a modern factory over opera and ballet and of a book of Albert Einstein over a Dostoyevski novel. For the advancement of man and culture, he felt, art also had to be "constructive"—that is, functional.

Now, fifty years later, it is still common to find that functional criteria are of prime importance in judging a building's worth. In a recent New York Times architectural page, a young modern architect described his design in classical functionalist terms—form expresses function: "It was a complex program, yet the house is remarkably simple, a rectangle that honestly expresses the program."[4]

As already mentioned, architects thought of as early functionalists such as Palladio, for example, still considered ornament an essential part of architecture. In fact, few unornamented buildings were built before the twentieth century. It is only in the present age that functional form stripped of "ornamental frippery," as Walter Gropius called it, has been pitted against nonfunctional, or ornamented, form. Despite all claims by modernists, setting these two opposites against each other was an arbitrary analytical device with no historical precedent. There is certainly nonessential stone in the ornamental columns of the Erectheum, but it is hard to imagine that the architect thought of the graceful caryatids as structural columns with applied ornament. The state of mind that separates ornamented from nonornamented form is alien to societies that do not share our compulsion for efficiency.

"Much time and labor is given up to aesthetic purposes" wrote anthropologist Bronislaw Malinowski in *Argonauts of the Western Pacific* "...there can be no doubt that the natives put their conscientiousness far beyond the limit of the purely necessary."[5]

Architectural ornament as a cultural symbol. Caryatides from the edition of Vitruvius by Fra Giacondo, Venice, 1511. The State of Caryae sided with the Persians against the Greeks. When the Greeks defeated the Persians, Caryae was conquered and the women carried off into slavery "without permitting them...to lay aside the long robes and other marks of their rank as married women, so that they might be obliged not only to march in the triumph but to appear forever as a type of slavery, burdened with the weight of their shame and so making atonement for their State." (Quote from Vitruvius, *De Architectura*, Book I)

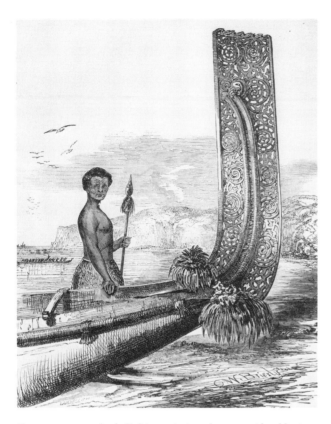

Contrary to popular belief, in societies where considerable time is spent on life-sustaining tasks, there is still a great amount of time devoted to "frivolous" nonfunctional tasks, such as ornamenting functional objects like this Maori canoe from New Zealand. (From the *London Illustrated News*, Oct. 4, 1851)

The line between useful and useless forms is hazy even in some Western countries. According to Luigi Barzini, the Italians feel that rationalizations for appearance are less important than the appearance itself. With cheerful abandon and charmingly deceitful results the Italians have long ignored the stern separation of function from ornament. As Barzini shows in *The Italians*, they have even gone so far as to excel in man-made imitations of one of the most beautiful of all natural ornaments—veined, colored marble:

> Since the earliest days local craftsmen have been unique in their ability to counterfeit the real thing. Half the marble one sees in churches or patrician "palazzi" is in fact but smooth plaster deceptively painted. *It is not necessarily always cheaper than the real thing: at times it can be infinitely more expensive and inconvenient. Of all the imitation marbles, Italians appreciate more those which really imitate nothing at all*, but create a combination of colours which never existed in nature. What is specially prized is the daring of their makers, their Promethian challenge to God.[6] [Author's emphasis]

The modern interpretation of functionalism did retain one rather irrational aspect of the traditional attitude: the utility of an object did not have to be real, it could be merely symbolic. Referring to the Red House designed by Phillip Webb in 1859 for William Morris, the noted historian Nikolaus Pevsner praised its proto-modern fireplace for being "completely devoid of any period allusions and completely functional in displaying its brick courses horizontally where the logs are laid and vertically where the smoke goes up."[7]

The Italians have always enjoyed artistry, whether or not it was "honest" in the sense of being an accurate representation of the facts. This facade in New York City includes a plaster wall painted to look like marble and a metal door (under the stairs) painted to look like wood.

A Catholic church with painted ornament in Tyrol, Austria.

The Machine Aesthetic

In the twentieth century, the principles of functionalism were said already to exist in the technology of the time. Architects had only to learn the lesson, as Le Corbusier wrote in *Aircraft* that "the world's miseries are due to the fact that functions are nowhere defined or respected."[8]

Machines epitomized function for the modernists. Not only were their forms bare and uncluttered by ornament, but they performed their specific tasks simply and efficiently. The aesthetic qualities of the machine—simplicity and geometry—became desirable in themselves, and the functionalism of the machine became the practical reason that architects used to explain their aesthetic preference. The machine-attribute of functionalism was associated with objects that resembled machines or machine products, whether or not these objects were actually functional in the same way as the machine. Thus in *Towards a New Architecture*, published in 1923, Le Corbusier compared the smooth walls of a modern house to sheet iron, its plain windows to those of a factory and concluded that one should be happy "having a house as serviceable as a typewriter."[9]

Yet this supposed advantage of modern functional forms—their serviceability or practicality—was often more illusory than real. The flat modern roof does offer another floor for living—a sun deck or terrace—but it also accumulates more snow than a traditional peaked roof and anyone who has built one knows it is much more difficult to waterproof. And although the flat roof gets rid of the dimly lit garret, it also deprives the occupants of "dead" attic space that is handy for storage and future expansion, not to mention insulation.

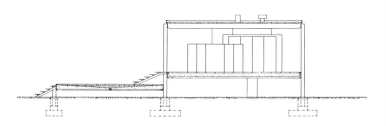

Section showing flat roof of Fox River House; Mies van der Rohe; 1946–1950. (From *Mies van der Rohe* by L. Hilberseimer. Paul Theobald and Company, publishers). The flat roof has become synonymous with modernism and hence with functionalism; however, it creates its own special problems of insulation and waterproofing.

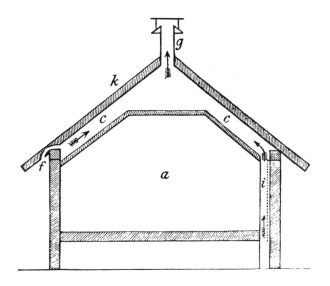

One inventive use of the so-called dead attic space that was cut away by modern architecture's flat roof: The height of the roof is used to create air circulation that ventilates the upper bedroom. (Drawing from *The Architecture of Country Houses* by A. J. Downing, 1850; Courtesy of the Avery Architectural Library, Columbia University)

One might believe that functional architecture would also be easier to maintain than traditional buildings. Yet maintaining large, flat stucco surfaces—the symbol of functional architecture of the twenties and thirties—is more difficult than taking care of less machinelike rough-cast plaster work or exterior surfaces broken up by ornament where normal weathering and cracks are less easily seen and the dust and dirt may even enhance the building's appearance.

Nor is the popular belief that functional design is cheaper than traditional design necessarily true. The open plan of the modern house, and its relatively larger areas of glass, has always been more expensive to heat and cool than traditional houses with "rooms" and smaller windows. The greater cost has only become more visible since the increase in fuel cost.

It was also alleged that modern buildings were more economical because they did away with non-useful, traditional ornament. The idea of an "economy" presumes that there is agreement as to what can be left out of a building while still satisfying both client and architect. This particular economy of modern architecture, omitting traditional, applied ornament, would have been inconceivable to previous generations of clients and architects for whom a building without ornament was as unthinkable as a brick wall without mortar. Because ornament was an essential part of a building it was impossible to think of a building costing more because it had ornament; without it the building would not have been a building. Ornament was included in the budget along with other necessary items like rafters, doors, windows, etc.

The modern movement changed this expectation; it arbitrarily defined ornament as anti-modern and thereby made it non-essential. By doing this, ornamented buildings seemed to become, *de facto*, more expensive. Now that ornament was no longer part of the standard package, it became an "extra."

Though, in the modern view, ornament is extra, it does not seem to cost any less to build without it. A house built today with traditional ornament will cost no more than a modern house, built in the same locale, without traditional ornament. The "extra" money spent in one house for traditional ornament will be spent in the other for modern "ornament." Because of the nakedness of its simplicity, modern detailing requires special care to execute satisfactorily.

Modern architects often attempt to reproduce smooth, functional machine surfaces in nonmachine materials; however, the effect of simplicity is difficult to achieve. Above, an effort to make a smooth plane ends up in showing each little misaligned brick. A less severe treatment in the same material, below, turns out to be more practical in that its irregularity disguises its imperfections.

Modernism's precision detailing is also costly. Most of the characteristic chrome and glass furniture with the "machine look" actually requires expensive hand finishing, and this is reflected in the price.

Another contention that has not been verified is that precise machinelike forms are easier and cheaper to mass-produce than ornamented or non-machinelike shapes. In Berlin in the late nineteen-twenties, manufacturers attempted to mass-produce square ceramic platters, but the necessary flatness and precision of the edges and corners were impossible to achieve on a mass-production basis. Out of a total production run, 5 percent were perfect, 5 percent were usable seconds and 90 percent had to be destroyed. The fact is that any mass-produced object is subject to minor imperfections and these are normally less noticeable if the form is complicated rather than simple.

One can also question the functional qualities of smaller objects of modern design. Handles in geometric curves or straight lines are no easier to hold than handles with complex curves. Baroque knives are as easily grasped as the Danish modern variety, and both will cut.

Ornamental and "functional"-looking knives. Both will cut. The modern knife right was designed by Jens H. Quistgaard. (Courtesy of Georg Jensen)

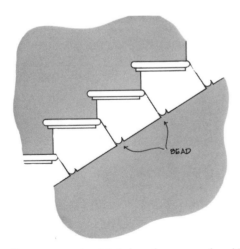

Detailing construction joints has always posed problems for architects. The apparent simplicity of modern detailing—with many of the joints carefully and honestly exposed—is often expensive because the slightest flaw in materials or workmanship is immediately noticeable.

Ornament was traditionally used to disguise these joints, as in the beading on these stone steps seen here in side view. When the stairs are completed, one will see only a half-round bead, not noticing that one of the recesses running beside it is actually a construction joint.

Form and Function

Modern functionalists assumed that the "honest" accommodation of function would result in a specific modern form without historical precedent. Not only should the form of an object or building express its function, but the form should be inevitably and uniquely determined by that function. Schools should look like schools, factories like factories and so on. Although it is arguable how successful modernists have been in this respect (except in the case of factories), the idea remains as strong as ever and persists among the general public as well. For example, a very common notion about the airplane is reflected in this quote from the September 17, 1973, issue of the *New Yorker* Magazine: "The jet airplane is perhaps the most beautiful of contemporary forms, and it derives its beauty from the immutable relationship between its form and its function—a plane flies because of its shape."

But there are few absolutes, even in aerodynamics, and airplanes will fly whether the motor is in the front or the back, or whether the wing is above, in the middle of or below the fuselage, or in all three positions. Airplanes will even fly if there is no body at all. But, given the comparatively limited number of different possible shapes of functioning airplanes, the ideal of form following function is still more applicable in aerodynamics than in architecture. Architectural requirements usually leave room for a wide variety of possible solutions to any given problem.

Consider a decision architects commonly have to make: how to limit the amount of sunlight that comes into a building. Some of the many ways to solve the problem are: brise-soleil—the concrete sun breakers made famous by Le Corbusier—venetian blinds, canvas awnings, shutters, roof overhangs and tinted glass. They are all "honest" and satisfactory solutions to light control, even though each has a different sense of style and evokes a different reaction in us because of its associations: the brise-soleil gives a brutally naked modern feeling, the tinted glass is sophisticatedly modern, window shades are cozy and old-fashioned and the awning is affable and traditional.

Since they are all practical solutions and none, with the possible exception of the brise-soleil, takes an inordinately large hunk of the budget, how does the architect decide which one to use? Assuming their equal availability, he picks the one that appeals to his sense of *style*. And yet, although it may seem obvious in this and other instances that the same function may be served equally well by several different styles, architects have claimed for nearly fifty years that functional criteria—that is, "meeting the needs of the architectural program"—determine the appearance of their buildings rather than aesthetic preferences. As already indicated, they have even gone so far as to claim that the true modern style was inevitable.

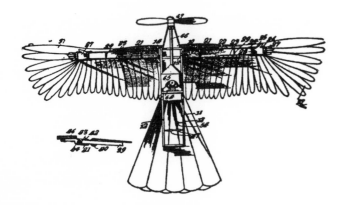

Patented flying machine, 1915. Even the exacting demands of aerodynamics allow for a wide variety of design choices. (Courtesy of Science and Technology Research Center, The New York Public Library. Astor, Lenox and Tilden Foundations)

The same function of regulating sunlight may be served by many different devices, each of which gives a different feeling because of the associations it evokes in us.

In the case of the different sun shading devices several forms serve one function, but the opposite is also true: one form can serve many functions. With often only minor modifications the basic form of the 150-year-old town house now serves many uses with equal ease: that of office building, theater, apartment building and single-family house. Similarly, part of a city may change over a period of time from residential to commercial, or to a mixture of uses, and not suffer thereby from a lack of "functionalism."

Eighteenth- and nineteenth-century town houses have proven to be among the most adaptable and sought-after forms of urban housing in this country as these three examples of a restaurant, movie theater and residence show.

The Functional Style

In a January 1950 special issue of the English journal *Architectural Review*, entitled "The Functional Tradition," the editors compared "functional" and "nonfunctional" objects and in the process clarified an interesting fact about the nature of modern functionalism. They used an example of two footbridges over a railroad track. The first bridge, which consisted of two lattice trusses forming handrails and supporting a footpath across the tracks, was described as good, functional design because, among other things, it was simple and was easily made from mass-produced products. The second bridge was considered bad, though it was the same bridge except for the simple addition of a roof. Its caption read: "A roof on the excellent bridge opposite merely results in [visual] boredom." The fact that the roof protected the commuter from the hostile elements while he crossed the tracks apparently did not interest the editors.

Clearly this was not a discussion about how well the bridges served their purpose. Nor did it hinge on how they were made; the same mass-produced parts formed both. The crux of the matter was what the bridges looked like and not how well they functioned. Once the real hierarchy of values is understood, there is no question as to which bridge is better and why. The first bridge is more beautiful to the modern eye; it is visually less cumbersome, simpler, more transparent, and the stark silhouette of the lattice trusses is not compromised by the visually heavy roof.

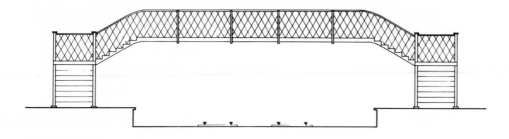

The first bridge, above, is considered functional primarily because of its visual simplicity. The same bridge with a roof, below, is called "boring." (Drawings from photographs in *Architectural Review*, January, 1950)

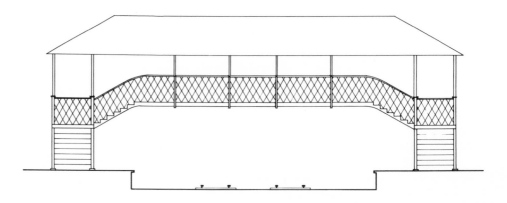

40

So we see that ultimately the modern criteria of excellence are stylistic rather than functional. Another example is the Versen spherical pendant lamp, which is one of the modern objects that Jay Doblin chose to include in his book *One Hundred Great Product Designs*. Although the lighting qualities of the lamp, designed in 1933, are mentioned, the emphasis of the discussion is clearly on its appearance: how the *hand-blown* globe was transformed into a perfect sphere; how its connection to the support was *minimized;* the delicacy of the support itself; and, finally, how the ceiling connection is *simplified* to the bare *minimum*. In the end, it is the lamp's styling that secured its place among the hundred greatest products.

There is some truth to the claim that function and technology play a part in style decisions, but it begs the question to stop there. We should realize by now that the blandness of modern architecture is far less a product of function or technical necessity than it is of arbitrary aesthetic choice.

The Versen spherical pendant lamp, 1933. Upon examination, the criteria that qualify this as a piece of "functional" design are not its ease of construction or its even distribution of light, but its simplicity and clean lines, which we have been conditioned to associate with something that serves its function well.

Simplicity

The modern preference for simplicity—visible in everything from the design of soup spoons to skyscrapers—is one of the most obvious characteristics of the movement and has had more serious consequences than the general blandness that typifies modernism. Love of simplicity has sometimes led designers to assume that the two-dimensional graphic clarity of a plan was a guarantee of the three-dimensional clarity of the final product. The author once sat through a design seminar in which two maps of Manhattan were shown during a discussion of the park system of New York City. One map had the existing parks, playgrounds and open spaces depicted in green, and, from several feet away, they looked like hundreds of small randomly spaced green specks dotting the island. The second map, which was proposed by a member of the seminar, had two large areas of green: Central Park and a mammoth proposed park area to the west and north of Central Park, dotted with buildings. The random specks of the first map were condemned as "cha-otic," whereas the graphic unity of the second was praised and described as "unified." The vital point omitted from the whole discussion was that people do not experience cities from the air, as we were doing in viewing the plans, but from ground level. Had we evaluated the park system as people actually see it while walking through the city, either plan could have been construed as "unified." The second map is unified in that it is in one lump, but the first map is also, by virtue of its recurring theme.

Simplicity of design also came to be equated with the basics of life. For example, at the Bridgewater Conference of the *Congrès International d'Architecture Moderne* in 1948, architect Aldo van Eyck spoke of the "overhaul of outworn values" resulting in a "universal revaluation towards the elementary."

However, the idea that the basic elemental needs of life can be satisfied by simple, elemental things is a dangerously simple misrepresentation. Some basic needs, such as an entrance to a shelter, may be simple to provide as well as universally

Entrance to an American middle-class home. The foyer is a "lock" big enough to stand in and take off one's coat and yet apart enough to prevent strangers from seeing into the private areas of the house.

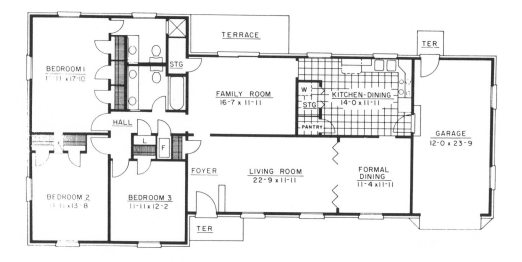

required, but once the bare necessity is there, a complex web of social and psychological needs related to that physical entrance remains to be sorted out. The needs differ considerably from group to group but satisfying them is one of the important requirements for a happy life.

For example, a small entrance foyer answers the need of most middle-class Americans. It is a place where coats are taken off and a "lock" to keep uninvited strangers out of the more private living areas. There is direct access from the foyer to the livingroom, but more restricted access to the family room and bedrooms.

Although superficially the same, there is a subtle difference in the entrance to the Danish middle-class home shown here. Instead of the living room door being the main door from the foyer, it is now one of several doors of equal importance, making the living room as separate from the entry as the bedrooms.

The traditional Chinese family home had a formal public courtyard adjacent to the street and a small receiving room for guests that was entirely separated from the internal family compound.

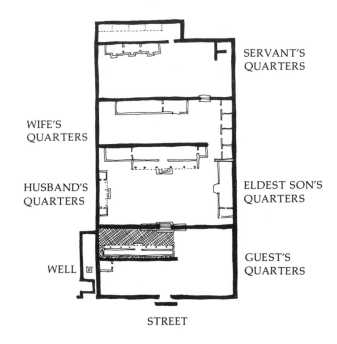

Entrance to a traditional Chinese home. The entry—an entire courtyard, with a guest room—is separated from the family area by a wall. (Courtesy of the Avery Architecture Library, Columbia University)

Entrance to a Danish middle-class home. A dormitory-type hallway emphasizes living room and bedroom doors equally. (Courtesy of Danish Ministry of Foreign Affairs, Copenhagen)

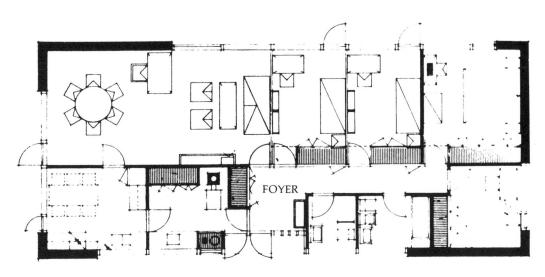

The well-to-do ancient Romans required large entrance courts because the retainers visiting them in the morning needed a gathering place away from the rest of the household. When the master was through with his morning bathing and breakfast, the retainers followed him to the forum for the day's business.

In the contemporary Yemeni house, the entrance is actually the entire interior stairway, which is sometimes seven stories high. The real division between the exterior and interior is not so much the doorway from the street to the house as the doorway from the stair landing to each floor.

Modern designers never looked beyond the mythical simplicity they espoused to the actual complex social realities that must be explored if architectural design is to accommodate people's needs. If the architect was happy, it was assumed that everyone else would be happy. "I propose one single building for all nations and climates," said Le Corbusier in 1937,[10] and modern architects proceeded to put this proposal into effect.

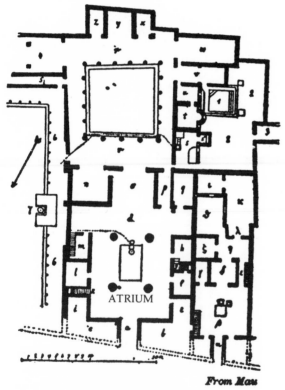

**HOUSE OF THE SILVER WEDDING
AT POMPEII**

Entrance to an ancient Roman home. The wealthier Roman needed a sizable entrance court because his entourage would gather there each morning before following him to the forum for the day's business. (Courtesy of the Avery Architectural Library, Columbia University)

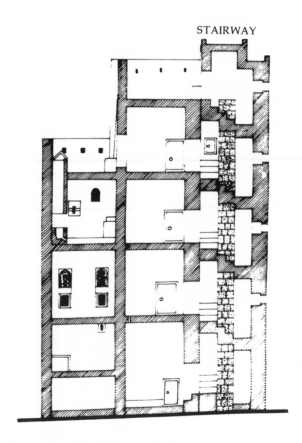

Entrance to a Yemeni home. The Yemeni home has a vertical entrance—sometimes seven stories high. As guests are taken to the top of the house via this stairway, they pass the closed doors of storage rooms, kitchen and living quarters. (Drawn by Marie Agnes Bertaud)

THE MISSIONARY ATTITUDE

The modern architect's personal vision is infused with a sense of moral superiority: "A question of morality; lack of truth is intolerable, we perish in untruth," wrote Le Corbusier in *Towards a New Architecture*.[11] The architect's mission is to redesign the world in his own image, and he has no doubt that his values apply to all. Certainly, he considers that less "civilized" peoples can only profit from adopting his way of life.

This view, as if he were surveying the rest of humanity from on high, is a legacy of Western colonialism. Colonization of the world was not only regarded as economically advantageous, but as a moral act. By introducing the savage to our civilization, we raised him to a higher plane of existence. To the missionary who followed upon the commercial colonization, the cultures he encountered were only anachronisms, to be eradicated through conversion.

The self-righteousness and sense of superiority that underlay colonialism stemmed partly from Christian teaching, which was represented as the *one* true religion to which all must be converted, and partly from the shift toward materialism brought on by the industrial revolution. "Civilization" had become measurable in material terms, and the West realized its phenomenal potential to produce signs of civilization in overwhelming quantities.

The modernist was the heir to this sense of superiority. The attitude he adopted toward people outside the movement was as patronizing as the South Seas missionary who set about teaching the "children of Paradise." And, like the missionary, he had his catechism. It consisted of certain ideological statements so often repeated and so seldom questioned that, as already mentioned, they achieved the status of "truths." More explicitly, these truths were:

Truth of Construction: The structure of a building should be clearly expressed, not disguised or falsified.

Truth of Materials: Materials used in construction should look like what they are. Concrete should not be painted; artificial materials should not imitate natural materials.

Truth of Form and Function: The shape of the building should be determined by what goes on inside it and not by the arbitrary whim of the architect.

Although these truths were represented as logical deductions from the spirit of the times, they were actually articles of faith, rhetorical statements whose moral overtones made them as unquestionable as Divine Law. Not all architects have adhered to the laws' letter, but these intimidating pronouncements have done more to determine the visual character of modern cities than any principle of architecture or planning based on more humane visual or social criteria.

Few participants in the drama of the modern movement's first years weighed these "truths" as wisely or objectively as Herman Muthesius. A German bureaucrat who was one of the first advocates of a new style in Germany, Muthesius described the first stirrings of modernism at the turn of the century and in doing so pin-pointed the weakness inherent in any claims of artistic truth:

In new departures, as is the case in this modern movement, the leading powers usually proceed from principles which they often send on ahead as programs, before their performances. The principle of truth, aimed against the alleged untruths of the preceding art, is rarely missing in such programs.... Fortunately, there are so many truths that such truth programs in art cannot be completely false.[12]

THE ENGINEER AND THE MACHINE

Because of the machine's smoothness and geometrical form, as well as its essential "functionality" it served as inspiration for modern forms. For his restraint and for the inevitable beauty of the machine, the engineer was applauded by modernists for showing the way toward good design.

As the superman of the nineteenth century, the engineer and his machines produced one astonishing feat after another. Because he fought and subdued the forces of Nature, his calculations were elevated to the level of Natural Law. It was understandable that the products of his calculations should become symbols of progress and of the ultimate superiority of Western culture.

Much romance attached to the engineer and his machines. Jules Verne took readers under the sea and literally out of the world in submarines and rockets, but it was J. K. Huysmans who, in his 1880 novel *A Rebours*, foretold the aura of sensualism associated with the machine that still dominates our century:

Nature . . . has had her day; she has finally and utterly exhausted the patience of sensitive observers by the revolting uniformity of her landscapes and skyscapes. . . . After all, to take what, among all her works, is considered to be the most exquisite, what among all her creations is deemed to possess the most perfect and original beauty—to wit, woman—has not man for his part, by his own efforts, produced an animate yet artificial creature that is every bit as good from the point of view of plastic beauty? Does there exist, anywhere on this earth, a being conceived in the joys of fornication and born in the throes of motherhood who is more dazzlingly, and more outstandingly beautiful than the two locomotives recently put into service on the Northern Railroad?[13]

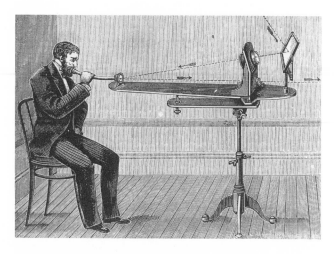

Alexander Graham Bell's photophone: One of the would-be marvels of the time, this was a device for translating sound into light that would be transmitted great distances and then turned back into sound, 1881. (Courtesy of The New York Public Library. Astor, Lenox and Tilden Foundations)

The feeling that anything could be accomplished by technology and the engineer led to great enthusiasm and some false starts. This aerial steam carriage was designed in 1843, but did not see service. (Courtesy of The New York Public Library. Astor, Lenox and Tilden Foundations)

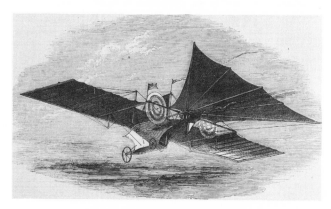

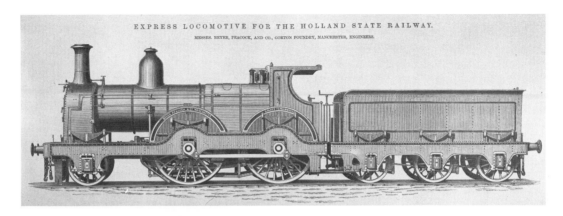

EXPRESS LOCOMOTIVE FOR THE HOLLAND STATE RAILWAY.

MESSRS. BEYER, PEACOCK, AND CO., GORTON FOUNDRY, MANCHESTER, ENGINEERS.

In the late nineteenth century the fascination with machine forms was so great that some found the locomotive more sensual than the female body. Above, locomotive: Holland State Railroad, 1881. (Courtesy of The New York Public Library. Astor, Lenox and Tilden Foundations) Below, nude: *September Morn* by Paul Chabas. (The Metropolitan Museum of Art, Purchase, Mr. and Mrs. William Coxe Wright Gift, 1957)

The lunar ship from Jules Verne's *De la Terre à la Lune*, 1870. The engineer could do everything, and what could not be done now would be done in the future. (Courtesy of The New York Public Library. Astor, Lenox and Tilden Foundations)

Machines held a magical appeal for the mind and the eye. They captivated the mind because, in an age that worshiped perpetual progress, they were the visible signs of that progress. They leveled mountains, spanned seas and conquered time. As early as the eighteen-forties, man, who before had been limited to a breakneck galloping speed at risk to life and limb, could now converse with his fellow passengers in relative safety while hurtling along at speeds of twenty to thirty miles an hour. Huge bridges effortlessly carried these speeding iron machines over great bodies of water: in 1850, the Britannia Bridge conquered the violent Straits of Menai with two spans of nearly five hundred feet each. It seemed that there was little that the engineer and his machines could not do.

While the mind was stunned by the feats themselves, the eye was captivated by the delicacy, grace and precise geometric beauty of these heralds of progress.

Machines embodied the most highly esteemed ethical values of the time; they were the essence of efficiency and economy. They were as simple as possible, geared to produce the most from the least and were the product of a methodical, rational approach. Machines and engineering works were the original "functional objects" that gave great satisfaction to modernists. A machine's sole purpose is to perform *a single* task. A locomotive pulls a payload along rails; a bridge gets people from one point to another over hostile elements; a power loom produces large quantities of fabric at low cost.

When the aim is to pull as many pounds of payload as possible, span the greatest distance or weave the most fabric, anything nonessential to the one task is naturally omitted. Hence the basic form of the locomotive, bridge or loom is simple relative to its task. Modern architects considered this direct relationship between form and function to be "honest," that is, the machine did not pretend to be something it was not. And they assumed that the function of a building could be as specifically defined as the function of a machine.

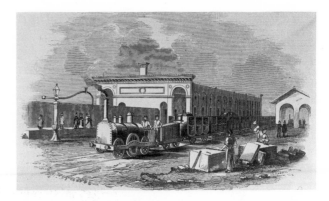

Early English passenger train in station, 1845. (Courtesy of The New York Public Library. Astor, Lenox and Tilden Foundations)

Prince Albert at the opening of Stephenson's tubular iron bridge over the Straits of Menai, 1852. Each span is nearly five hundred feet long. The bridge is still used by British Railways. (Courtesy of The New York Public Library. Astor, Lenox and Tilden Foundations)

Slowly, through a mixture of morality, practicality and the disgust at bourgeois taste, the aesthetic of precise machine forms gained prestige. As early as 1859, the English philosopher Herbert Spencer had equated the machine aesthetic with the advancement of civilization when he criticized the inferior curves of a Chinese junk compared to the superior rigid arcs and taut surfaces of the machine: "A Chinese junk, with all its contained furniture and appliances, nowhere presents a line that is quite straight, a uniform curve or a true surface," he wrote in *First Principles*, characterizing such "defects" as typical of the "productions of the less-advanced nations."[14]

The Chinese junk, with its hand-hewn delicately curved timbers, was considered inferior to the straight lines and "true surfaces" of machine-made products, such as the shuttleless loom in the next illustration. The differences between machine precision and handmade irregularity were considered indicative of the superiority of Western culture. (Courtesy of The New York Public Library. Astor, Lenox and Tilden Foundations)

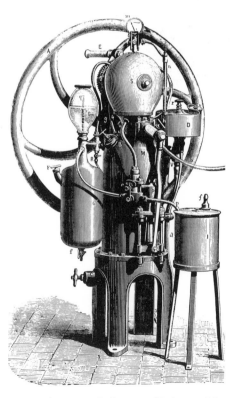

Machines were the original "functional" objects. Like most other machines, this 1881 soda water machine had one and only one function. (Courtesy of The New York Public Library. Astor, Lenox and Tilden Foundations)

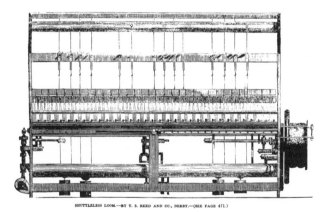

SHUTTLELESS LOOM.—BY T. S. REED AND CO., DERBY.—(SEE PAGE 471.)

Shuttleless loom, 1851. (Courtesy of The New York Public Library. Astor, Lenox and Tilden Foundations)

The Rational Method

Modern architecture's restrained, precise forms are supposedly three-dimensional realizations of a cool, objective reasoning process. The great engineering triumphs of the nineteenth century provided the examples to be followed.

The engineer dealt rationally with absolutes; when his towers, tunnels or steamships mastered nature, it was the inexorable march of the rational scientific method, the clear manifestation of progress that everyone had come to expect. The engineer's rational approach, based on the practicality demanded by his working context, centered in asking the question "Why?" The habit of asking that practical question led to the expectation of a practical answer. And certainly in the realm of physical forces it was reasonable to expect practical answers. Ex.: Q. Why does the bridge collapse? A. Because the train was too heavy.

The modern architect viewed his own problems in the light of the engineer's successes, and it seemed to him that by adopting the same rational method based on the same practical values, he too could achieve inevitably correct solutions. So he adopted this method with a vengeance. Unfortunately, as we have seen and will continue to find, the architect's realm includes not only physical forces, but also cultural associations, perceptions and such impractical factors as beauty, which do not easily submit to the rigors of reason. The simple question "Why?" is seldom sufficient. Nevertheless, armed with the tool of "rational justification," the architect ruthlessly scrutinized every aspect of building and where there was no apparent reason for an item, it was summarily discarded.

Rationalism and the Engineer

Placing great emphasis on their "rational method," modern architects reasoned that art, like physics, had immutable laws that if pursued rationally would lead to modern forms.

But what is a rational method? In fact, one can only argue rationally after one has chosen a set of values from which to argue. The way these values are chosen is as important and revealing as the

rigor of the rational method used later to implement them. Depending on his initial premises, for example, a planner could arrive rationally at either a grid or a nongrid plan for a city. However, when studying buildings and cities, one is seldom patient enough to seek out these underlying values and analyze the plan to see if it does follow logically from them. Thus when the grid plan is called "rational" without an analysis of its context and premises, it probably means that the values of economy, efficiency and simplicity that it repre-

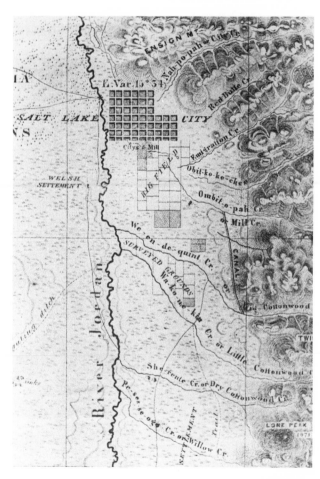

The grid plan of Salt Lake City no doubt seems reasonable and rational because we are familiar with the values of economy, efficiency and simplicity that it embodies. (Courtesy of The New York Public Library. Astor, Lenox and Tilden Foundations)

sents are considered desirable. An "irrational" plan or building is often simply one whose premises are considered unacceptable.

The values on which the modern movement's ideology was based were chosen with an intense emotion and poeticism and not with the objectivity that their professed reliance on reason suggests.

The choice of reason as the determining factor in architectural design grew out of an idolization of the engineer and his use of the rational method. Having abandoned the established rules of historical styles, the architect needed to have a new rationale for design decisions. By aligning himself with the engineer he acquired a ready-made set of

rules: the objective, methodical approach of science. Architects fancied themselves restricted by the same severe limitations as the engineer who designed precision tools within extremely tight economic and technical requirements. More importantly, it was believed that these were the rules that epitomized the spirit of the modern world.

In *New Architecture and the Bauhaus* in 1953, Walter Gropius drew a parallel between architecture and engineering techniques in industry, claiming that "the direct affinity between the tight economy of space and material in industry and [architectural] structures based on these principles is bound to condition the future planning of our towns." The principles to which he refers are those that, in the popular view, described the engineer's work: "It [a modern building] must be true to itself, logically transparent and virginal of lies or trivialities, as befits a direct affirmation of our contemporary world of mechanization and rapid transit."[15]

Although in the end, Le Corbusier and Gropius considered the architect to be something more than an engineer, Le Corbusier felt that engineers, through their impartial calculations, had established the only proper starting point for architecture.

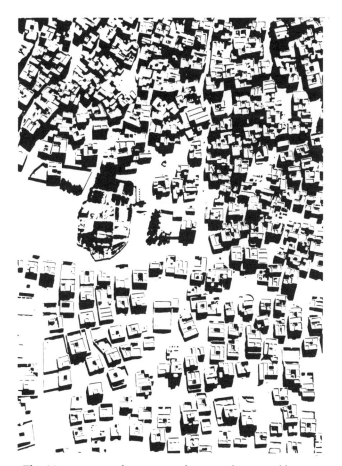

This Yemeni town plan appears chaotic and irrational because we do not understand the family and tribal value structure that gave rise to it. (Drawn by Alain Bertaud)

A perspective view of a project for a skyscraper city by Ludwig Hilberseimer, 1927. "...the direct affinity between the tight economy of space and material in industry and structures based on these principles is bound to condition the future planning of our towns."—Walter Gropius, 1935.

Rationalism and the Machine

The engineer's rational approach was considered a way to achieve "truth" and an almost mystical consonance with cosmic forces. But the admiration of the machine also had more subtle effects. Because of its rational origin, the machine was associated with the laws of nature that were knowable only through reason. This, in turn, led architects to assign moral qualities to the machine: it was considered "noble," "fundamental"—in the sense of reflecting "first principles"—and an "honest" expression of the times. Gradually these moral qualities were transferred to objects and buildings that looked like machines, that is, that were visually simple, lacked ornament, had geometric rather than free-form shapes and that did not visually refer to historical precedents.

The orderliness that science and reason implied was reinforced by the neatness and clarity of the machines of the period. Shown here is a trunk detail from a 1931 eight-liter Bentley. Ironically, then as now, this fine machined appearance is more often than not achieved by costly hand finishing. (Courtesy of Edgar A. Jurist, Vintage Car Store, Nyack, N.Y.)

The orderliness that science and reason implied was reinforced by the orderly appearance of machines. Their visual clarity was as important as the fact that they were the physical manifestations of the rational process, and so enamored were architects of their proportions, masses and materials that machines came to be regarded as real works of art. Although the delight in machines goes far back in history, the degree to which machines dictated the aesthetic norm in the early years of this century was unique. Even the beauties of the past were interpreted in machine terms, as when Le Corbusier referred to the marble temples of ancient Greece as "plastic machinery" giving the impression of "naked polished steel."[16]

The most incisive explanation of the poetic influence of reason on aesthetic preferences came from the distinguished Mexican painter Angel Zarraga at the Paris Exhibition of decorative arts in 1925:

To painters of my generation the intersection of two planes produces a pleasure of a different type, but similar in quality, to that which a modulation of a soft green and violet might produce in the neo-impressionist generation. Negro [primitive] sculpture, possibilities of concrete, naval architecture, the architecture of airplanes, all these possibilities and inventions, plus the famous "everything consists of cylinders, cones and spheres" [Cézanne] contribute to the profound modification of our sensitivity, and give us a taste for the solid form. From this point, to imagining that our sense of reason commands, is only a step further. We took that step.... Thus it is the total expression of a sensitivity conditioned by new psychological stimuli, which tries to express, to convey, the generation from 1919–1925. These stimuli have been enumerated by the artists themselves: science, with its relativism and its fairy-tale beauty, the movies, electricity, and speed—"A new beauty with which the Universe has enriched itself..." With great rapidity, we have helped to replace animal forms with new mechanical forms.[17]

Le Corbusier compared the plastic quality of the Doric temple, shown above, with the polished steel of the modern machine, as, for example, the 1917 Benz six-cylinder aircraft engine below. (Courtesy of Science and Technology Research Center, The New York Public Library. Astor, Lenox and Tilden Foundations)

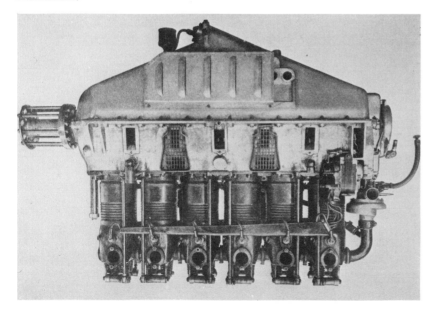

Standardization

Actively discouraging a diversity of architectural styles, modernists set about trying to standardize (or "rationalize") the building industry according to a set of principles that would create a consistent modern architecture throughout the world. Architecture was not to reflect human or cultural differences, but rather the social homogeneity that mass-production technology had allegedly brought about. As Le Corbusier saw it, a "mass-production spirit" had to be created: "The spirit of constructing mass-production houses. The spirit of living in mass-production houses. The spirit of conceiving mass-production houses."[18]

Some modernists, among them the de Stijl group—early Dutch proponents of the modern style—looked to man-made materials like reinforced concrete to eliminate the personal character that craftsman-formed materials like brick, stone and wood lent to a building.

Through the adoption of standardization and mass-production techniques, modern architecture would create impersonalized monotonous cityscapes devoid of the strong individualistic touch of the designer—intentionally. In fact, Gropius felt that such standardization could only come after the designer's personal mark had been suppressed.

Above all, architecture was to be objective. Gropius claimed that the restrictions of mass production would not totally eradicate individual expression because by manipulating the depersonalized, standardized elements, the designer could achieve diversity. To prove this was possible he cited situations in the past where "standardization" has resulted in uniform appearance but some retention of visual variety. Although he is not specific, he probably had in mind one of the examples of indiginous architecture so popular among the modernists because of their simplicity, such as Greek fishing villages. However, the inherent fallacy here is that modern standardization has a ruthless precision inconceivable before machine production. In picturesque Greek villages, windows that look alike from a distance often differ slightly at closer view because they were made by different craftsmen at different times, and as Ruskin pointed out nearly a century ago, such slight irregularities make the elevations more lively; the eye senses them and almost involuntarily scans the facades, searching them out. It is exactly these subtle, eye-catching un-machinelike variations that mass production has ironed out. The razor-sharp definition of machine-made products is qualitatively different from what Gropius referred to as the standardization of the past.

Mass production was expected to produce a regularity little different from the "standardization" of the past. However, the precision made possible by the machine permits a regularity that is qualitatively different from the standardization of the past. Above, a Greek fishing village (photo by John Zeisel); below, apartment buildings in New York City.

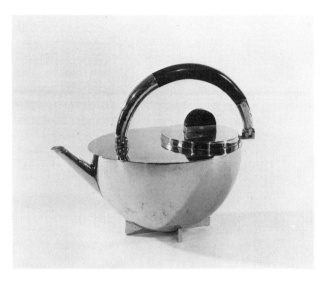

Mass production does not automatically result in machinelike forms. In fact, how an object is made does not necessarily determine what it looks like. The geometric forms of the teapot above were produced by hand, whereas the pitcher with the voluptuous curves below was mass produced. The teapot, 3⅝" high and of nickel silver and ebony, was designed by Marianne Brandt in 1924 and manufactured by the Bauhaus Metal Workshop in Germany. Collection, The Museum of Modern Art, New York; Phyllis B. Lambert Fund. The pitcher was designed by Eva Zeisel.

ROMANTICISM

The Romantic movement had spent itself by the mid-nineteenth century, yet some of its ideas, such as the role of genius and originality in art, persist to the present day.

By virtue of the Romantic movement the artist was elevated to a higher plane than he had ever enjoyed in the past. Previously, a great artist had been felt to be divinely inspired, a conduit for a vision greater than his own. The artist's genius lay in the fact that he possessed, to an exceptional degree, the same talent that others had to a lesser degree. The difference between artist and craftsman was quantitative.

On the other hand, the Romantic artist came to be considered the source of his own inspira-

Reverence for the rational method permeated all aspects of life, and Sherlock Holmes was the classical rationalist. Dr. Watson's assumption that rationalism and cold precision go hand in hand is reminiscent of the modern movement: "All emotions . . . were abhorrent to his cold, precise but admirable balanced mind. He was, I take it, the most perfect reasoning and observing machine that the world has seen . . ."—from A. Conan Doyle, *A Scandal in Bohemia*. (Illustration courtesy of General Research and Humanities Division, The New York Public Library. Astor, Lenox and Tilden Foundations)

tion; he drew upon his own inner resources. His gift was a unique spiritual vision that allowed him to perceive reality in a way in which an ordinary man could not. It was a qualitative rather than a quantitative difference.

With this new emphasis on individuality came a similar emphasis on originality as a prerequisite for artistic greatness. The present connotation of "original" in art, meaning roughly without precedent, is recent, dating from the beginnings of the Romantic movement, as the Oxford English Dictionary demonstrates in two of its definitions:

3. Produced by . . . some thing or person directly; underived, independent 1792. 4. Such as has not been done or produced before; novel or fresh in character or style 1756.

The artist's vision was necessarily original because it was felt to come from his own inner perceptions. The Romantics placed great emphasis on personal experience, and the artist's inner vision, molded by his unique experiences, would naturally differ from artist to artist. In other words, his work would be original. The degree of originality would depend on the depth of the artist's genius.

If an artist was imitative, or followed the rules by which the common people defined beauty, he must, by definition, lack originality and therefore be incapable of great art. Because of this, anyone who pandered to popular taste was considered a workman rather than an original, creative artist. The true artist rejected the popular definition of beauty and conceived his own, thus setting himself apart from society. He became a rebel.

In our century the view of the artist separated from society has become commonplace and we assume it to have been the condition of the artist throughout history, when in fact it was not. Vasari, for example, in *Lives of the Artists*, describes how the public and his fellow artists responded to the exhibition of one of Leonardo's paintings. "Men and women, young and old" flocked to see it, "as if they were attending a great festival." We, however, have been conditioned by the Romantic idea that the artist betrays his individuality if he accepts the popular idea of beauty.

Perpetuating the nineteenth-century Romantic ideal of the rebel-artist genius, modernists rejected the popular preference for eclectic architecture that had dominated the nineteenth and early twentieth centuries and shocked their contemporaries by saying that the mansions of the industrial barons were ugly while their factories were beautiful.

Modern architects have had diverse views on beauty since the nineteen-twenties. The technocrats still feel that the mass-produced machine-made look is the most beautiful, but another group favors the rustic shed or barnlike look and a third finds beauty in shopping centers and commercial architecture. Still other architects prefer forms without historical associations, abstractions that are beautiful because of their modernity.

All of these extreme choices share one essentially negative aspect: they represent a style that is not "popular" in the sense of being desired by the majority of people. In this respect, the architects seem to have espoused and perpetuated the nineteenth-century Romantic position that someone who accepts the popular rules of beauty lacks originality and creativity and, lacking these, cannot be an artist.

The non-architect's popular conception of beauty may include different aspects of each of the four choices just mentioned: some factory elements may be considered beautiful, or shopping centers or barns or abstract forms. But they are popularly acceptable only in their context. That is, some barns may be beautiful, but only as long as they remain barns, not when they become houses; likewise some factories may be beautiful but only as factories, not when the factory elements are used in houses. To break away from the popular ideal, modernists have taken these things out of their original acceptable contexts, building houses that look like barns, factories or scaleless abstractions. With the exception of an indoctrinated elite, few other people show any interest in this intentional violation of the vulgar idea of beauty, but instead, the overwhelming majority chooses to live in the traditional, eclectic suburban house.

EVOLUTION

Rejecting the past was the starting point for modern architecture. The several factors inherent in this rejection can be reviewed as follows:

1. Architects felt that they could decisively affect people's lives and behavior through changes in the physical surroundings.

2. There was a belief in Progress and Change that made the past and its traditions seem irrelevant.

3. There was also a belief that by eliminating those elements in buildings that served no practical purpose, such as ornament, architecture could function in harmony with the laws of nature.

All of these ideas were brought to architecture in part through an imperfect understanding of evolutionary theory.

According to the popular, though erroneous, interpretation of the theory of evolution, there was scientific proof that progress was inevitable and society was forever moving toward something better. Evolutionary theory postulated that species were continually adapting to their surroundings through the perpetuation of advantageous mutations, and as the species evolved toward a more perfect form, useless organs, or species, withered away. It was the law of nature and beyond man's control; man could only marvel and submit.

The popular interpretation of evolution had led to the belief that, biologically at least, the past was obsolete. Only the paleontologist needed to look back—not the man interested in the present or future. Applying this oversimplification to architecture, the modernist found scientific justification for ignoring traditional styles. He abandoned the past and made the crucial claim that the architectural traditions that had gone before—with all their complex social implications—were as irrelevant as the sloth's fourth toe. As the Italian Futurist architect Sant' Elia wrote in 1914, modern architecture could not "be subject to any law of historical [stylistic] continuity."[19]

The popularized notions about evolution also encouraged belief in a unique modern style. If, as postulated, there was a tendency for new forms to evolve to meet new needs, then architectural forms that had worked in the past would be inadequate for present needs. Although it grossly underestimated the value of our past and present associations with our surroundings, this view offered a simple and apparently scientific justification for developing an independent "modern" style.

The theory of evolution also supported the well-entrenched concept of economizing action and, therefore, functionalism. Since life itself was guaranteed by the elimination of all but the essential, why shouldn't the architect's choices be guided by the same principle? The sleekness of modern architecture was the result of paring away unnecessary forms, just as the evolutionary process slowly removed unnecessary limbs and organs. The march of modernism tended to be thought of in terms of the process of natural selection.

A seventeenth-century sketch of the extinct dodo. According to evolution, useless species were fated to disappear. (Courtesy of Art and Architecture Division, The New York Public Library. Astor, Lenox and Tilden Foundations)

Anti-Historicism and the Spirit of the Times

The Romantic movement had made the artist a voluntary exile from popular taste, so that he was a rebel on one hand, but a potential leader on the other. The architects of the early modern movement in particular felt it their duty to lead the masses out of their ignorance by establishing new standards in architectural design and planning that the common man would accept once he saw their inherent logic. They were supported in their position by the popular interpretation of Darwinism and the sense of inevitable improvement accompanying each technological advance. All these elements conspired to reinforce the most destructive of the modern ideological tenets: its anti-historicism.

The rallying point for the new architecture was the denunciation of the old. Architects tore themselves loose from the roots of tradition to move freely in the new world of their own making. In *Towards a New Architecture* in 1923, Le Corbusier heralded the beginning of a new epoch and spirit, to be noted especially in industrial production. Traditional architecture, he said, was stifling and the old styles "a lie."[20] Twenty-five years later at the Bridgewater Conference of CIAM Aldo van Eyck, a second-generation modernist echoed the cry, claiming "A new civilization is being born." In the nineteen-seventies the third generation of modernists persists in claiming that traditions are dead and a new social order has replaced them.

Modernists believed that unique architectural forms, appropriate to the modern era, would evolve from the universally sensed "spirit of the times." By definition, the "appropriate" style would be the one that used the newest materials and techniques to make new and different architectural forms rather than the same new materials and techniques to make traditionally based forms. How the "spirit" worked was not clearly defined, but it was invoked often enough to merit some inquiry into exactly what it implied.

According to the modernists, life had changed to such an extent due to technology that man can only acknowledge his new condition by a total change in the form of his surroundings or be doomed to suffocate in the past. As the spokesman for the new "spirit," the architect would educate the masses and lead the way, showing them the proper forms for modern times.

The "spirit of the times" was the pervading influence guiding the architect's decisions. At the very least, it could be consulted in order to arrive at one solution that was more appropriate than another; at most, it presided over a miraculous "natural" growth, free of man's haphazard will, toward the inevitable outcome. Walter Gropius, in *The New Architecture and the Bauhaus* in 1935, spoke of the forms of the New Architecture as differing from traditional forms in that "they are not the personal whims of a handful of architects avid for innovation, at all cost, but simply the inevitable logical product of the intellectual, social and technical conditions of our age."[21]

Traditionally the architect, or master mason, had been guided by his knowledge of what buildings had looked like and how they had been planned in the past. Precedent, plus the limitations of materials, techniques and other practical restrictions were responsible for the relatively clear definition of the building's form. Originality was by no means precluded; there was considerable latitude within these limits. But when traditional styles were abandoned, architects no longer had these reference points, and there was no longer any guide lines to indicate the correct aesthetic choices. A new authority was needed to fill the void, and the all-pervasive "spirit of the times" fit the role. It had two invaluable advantages for the makers of the new tradition: It was inevitable and ambiguous—at once inescapable and yet open to a wide range of interpretation.

The Universal Style

After declaring the inevitability of the modern style, members of the movement assumed that the public would recognize and embrace it. Instead, modernism has remained an elitist movement, aesthetically inaccessible to the majority. The biggest inroads modernism has made in the common man's private life have been limited to kitchen and bathroom design.

By declaring the appropriateness of their architecture, and theirs alone, modernists placed themselves in opposition to the overwhelming majority of potential home owners, particularly in this country. When they assumed that visual traditions were no longer a valuable part of people's lives, they automatically excluded themselves from a major environmental undertaking—the planning of suburbia. Architects yielded this realm to nonarchitects largely because of their unwillingness to design houses based on traditional styles and to plan large groupings of detached single-family houses.

A cast-iron warehouse in New York City built circa 1880 has traditional elements of trabeated Western architecture.

Warehouse in New York City. Technical capabilities were sometimes used as a rationale for the modern style. The continuous ribbon window was exploited because new structural techniques did away with the need for structural walls. Starrett-Lehigh Building; Russel G. and Walter M. Corry, architects; Yatsuo Matsui, associated architect; 1931.

Michelangelo's facades for the Campidoglio, Rome, employed a significant innovation within the Greco-Roman architectural tradition. They had pilasters that extended for two full stories rather than one-story pilasters with a different architectural order for each story.

III.

Social Ills and the Environment

London slums in an engraving by Gustave Doré. (Courtesy of The New York Public Library. Astor, Lenox and Tilden Foundations)

Evolution also postulated that the physical environment was an indirect factor determining a species's characteristics. Looking at the wretched social and physical conditions in nineteenth-century industrial cities from this point of view, we readily see the logic in the assumption that the horrifying social conditions had been caused by miserable physical situations. It was believed that you would remove the cause of the social ills by getting rid of the narrow streets and sunless yards. Influenced by John Ruskin's proposal of "groups of well-proportioned houses" with "clean and busy street[s] within an open country without" (see Ruskin's collected lectures in *Sesame and Lilies*) and the presentation of William Morris's Utopia, from which industrial cities themselves were banished, designers and social reformers of the time equated physical cleanliness and large open spaces with social well-being. The belief advanced by modern architects that form can determine behavior stems from these sources.

In 1898, Ebenezer Howard, a clerk in the city of London, published what became one of the most influential books in modern city planning—*Tomorrow*, later known as *Garden Cities of Tomorrow*. Outlining an approach to city planning that was supposed to cure most of the problems of modern cities, the author suggested building independent towns or "garden cities" in the countryside that would be of limited size and have within them all the necessary industry, business and cultural facilities to be self-sufficient. This idea has decisively influenced modern planning and architecture, but in retrospect it seems comprised of a strange mixture of moralism, pragmatism and optimism. It is a classic example of the simplistic cause-and-effect relationship seen between behavior and environment that still dominates planning and architecture and that lulled modern architects into believing that they could change the way people live by modifying their physical surroundings. Howard himself rather quaintly felt that "restoring the people to the land" would "pour a flood of light on the problems of intemperance, of excessive toil, of restless anxiety, of grinding poverty—the true limits of Governmental interference, ay, and even the relations of man to the Supreme Power."[22]

The apartment block surrounded by parks and abundant sunlight and air—the outgrowth of the nineteenth-century interpretation of evolutionary philosophy and Howards' garden city idea—has become the hallmark of modern architecture.

Towers in parks are contemporary spinoffs from the garden city ideal.

THE SOCIAL CONCERN OF THE MODERN MOVEMENT

Although the theoreticians of the nineteen-twenties and nineteen-thirties were often vague about how to accomplish specific social aims, they wanted to mitigate the deplorable urban conditions brought about by industrialization. They sought to "modernize" man, to bring him into "harmony" with the times, which meant eliminating reminders of the past that inhibited the progress of modern life. Their improvements could include anything from straightening out the narrow winding streets of old cities that slowed speeding cars to replacing three- and four-story housing with apartment towers in order to allow more land for open space. Bringing the advantages of industrial society to more people was an admirable goal, but the way the proponents of the modern movement attempted it has been destructive.

As already suggested, the ideology of modern architecture has tended to deal with how people should live rather than how they do live; it has set out to redefine social as well as aesthetic values. When traditional social patterns did not conform to their modern idea of how buildings, streets and cities should be used, designers ignored them, justifying this omnipotent approach with the stated belief that everyone in the world has the same basic social and physical needs.

Professional habit reinforced the modernists' assumption that the design should reflect the architect's hierarchy of aesthetic and social values, regardless of who the client was. In the past, clients had chosen one architect over another because he was esteemed by the general public, and the architect's aesthetic decisions were accepted because he was an acknowledged expert.

Architectural decisions affecting the social life of the client were also governed by long-standing tradition, and the architect made these choices more or less unconsciously. Such decisions involved the client's concept of privacy and were reflected in his perception of space; they could determine, to take the most common examples: 1. The placement of windows: If they overlook the street, they offer an opportunity for contact between street activities and the house. 2. The placement of doors: Whether they open into formal or informal areas of the house is important and depends on whether the client entertains business guests (formally) or family and close friends (informally). 3. The placement of rooms within the house: Is a separate dining area needed for formal entertaining; do the parents' sense of privacy demand that each child have a separate bedroom or is it acceptable to have several children in one room? These decisions also affect the community since they regulate the relationship among the individual houses or apartments, and the relationships of the dwellings to public spaces. The same kinds of decisions obviously promote or interfere with behavior patterns in offices, theaters, parks and playgrounds.

In pre-industrial society the architect either intuitively understood his client's needs, because they were similar to his own, or these needs were codified by tradition and the architect had only to follow the custom. But with the onset of industrialization the architect-client relationship took on a new aspect. In large-scale projects, the client who paid for the project—often a government agency—was not the client who would use the project, and this separation between the paying-client and the user-client was critical. Not only did architects no longer have the direct contact with the user-client that had been common in the past, but more importantly, because the user-client now often came from a different class or even a different culture, the architect was often unaware of cultural differences between his own and his client's perception of space—that is, the different ways that he and his user-client would choose to behave in the same room.

Ignoring these cultural differences and making choices based on their own experience, most modern architects assumed that the user-clients would become accustomed to living the way they expected them to live. In doing this, far from feeling that they were bypassing their clients' actual preferences, they actually considered that they were fulfilling their social responsibilities to them. For was it not incumbent on them to lead people away from wrong-headed particular views to a more universal design for living, which would be consonant with the advanced stage of modern technology and lead to a better life?

It is evident from the world-wide uniformity of modern architecture that the universal approach promoted by the architect allowed his own values to be consistently dominant and cultural differences to disappear by virtue of the supposed homogeneity of modern times.

In 1927 Gropius had encouraged the establishment of universal minimum standards of housing based on his anticipation of the "impending equalization of life requirements under the influence of travel and world trade."[23] However, cultural differences have not disappeared. Every wall and window has a social as well as an aesthetic implication, and this implication differs from class to class and from culture to culture. To the working class family, the front window is what the telephone is to the middle class family: a means of direct communication with the community. Things are passed through it; people talk from it. In other words, the street outside is considered an extension of the living space inside. In a middle-class suburb, on the other hand, the street is not an extension of the house, and the front window may not even open. It is primarily a social control device, showing the neighbors that you "belong" by your display of the proper symbols.

There are many other examples of culturally different perceptions of space. When Algiers became independent, the Algerians moved into the high-rise buildings that had been built for the French, but instead of using the rooms as they had been intended, they removed all the doors and broke through many walls in an effort to open up the living spaces. Whereas the Europeans had required physical barriers to insure their privacy, the Algerians preferred large open spaces, having other means of insuring the privacy of their family. One way was not to invite strangers into the household in the first place.

Window as symbolic means of communication.

Window as actual means of communication.

The success of any past or present design solution depends on whether or not the people who use it will actually share the values that the design embodies. Occasionally, when this happens the design is completely successful. In the late nineteen-twenties Clarence Perry proposed the "neighborhood unit" as a planning principle for middle-class communities in this country. It consisted of a residential area of limited size, bounded by traffic arteries, with a center space containing community facilities and an elementary school that was attended by all the children living in the unit. Pedestrian and auto traffic were separated. The houses faced onto lawns and public walkways, and cars approached the houses from the rear via driveways that had direct access to the peripheral roads. Thus children's play areas were kept free from auto traffic. At least part of the success of this idea was due to the fact that it embodied the values of the middle classes for whom it was intended. When the same principles were applied in the planning of Chandigarh, India, they met with notable failures. (See Ch. 4.)

Radburn, New Jersey, 1929. A design for a middle-class community that takes into consideration middle-class values.

The Bauhaus Social Program

Founded in 1919 by Walter Gropius, the Bauhaus remained a center for all facets of modern design education until 1933. During that period it developed the most coherent, systematic approach to the planning, design and construction of what Gropius called the "New Architecture." The sociological requirements of the modern living unit formed one aspect of this approach.

The Bauhaus claimed to have a scientific basis for identifying and accommodating people's social needs in its sociological approach. Its major finding, which was in fact, neither sociological nor scientific, was the supposed "minimum sociological requirement" for every person. However, social needs are not quantifiable in the way that this postulate suggests. This concept of "minimum" requirements, which shows the continuing influence of "economizing action," was an economic category erroneously applied to human needs; it was ideology rather than sociology.

Gropius made several pronouncements that were intended as sociological justifications for his architectural solutions: 1. People have no natural attachment to the ground. 2. People erroneously find larger apartments desirable. 3. Although single-family houses are the most desirable, they are not a practical solution to modern housing needs. 4. There are cultural advantages to high-rise apartments because of the increased possibility of meeting people.

Since Gropius made these statements, much evidence has shown that none of them is necessarily true: 1. An example in the next chapter of an Indian city designed by Europeans demonstrates that, in some cases at least, people who are accustomed to having some small piece of land adjacent to their home—even if it is only the street—suffer considerable strain and inconvenience if they are deprived of it. 2. It is an arbitrary imposition of values for the architect to say that people are mistaken to like larger apartments. 3. Ignoring the single-family house as a design possibility amounts to the dismissal of the suburbs as a potential solution to urban problems. 4. Increasing the potential for contact does not necessarily increase the number of actual contacts. Since Gropius wrote about this aspect of modern life, the anonymity of high-rise apartment buildings has become legendary.

Gropius's concluding pronouncement was that every adult should have his own room, no matter how small it might be. According to studies of culturally different perceptions of privacy, a German wanting to be "alone" must be in the room alone with the door closed, but this would not be true for Puerto Ricans or East Indians, for example, whose perception of privacy does not require such a distinct physical separation. Thus Gropius's minimum social requirement is, at best, the generalization of a specific cultural trait.

THE TECHNOLOGICAL IMPERATIVE AND THE "OPEN PLAN"

Steel and reinforced concrete column and slab construction made possible the unobstructed "open planning" and "flowing spaces" that later became the familiar trademark of modern architecture: the wall was no longer necessary because it no longer had a structural role. This constructional change was considered an outstanding achievement by such modern architects as Gropius. What was never mentioned and went unnoticed, however, was the impact of this open plan on the social life of the house's occupants. Without any demonstrable need, new social relationships came to be defined by technological, economic and aesthetic criteria. When the wall between the living room and the dining room is taken away, it becomes difficult to have two separate activities going on simultaneously. This is acceptable in a middle-class family where the man and wife share their social life, but less so in working-class families where social life centers on separate men's and women's peer groups. And in the Middle East, for example, where informal family life and formal entertaining of guests should never overlap, it is even less acceptable.

In its most extreme form, in Mies van der Rohe's houses, the open plan meant abolishing all privacy except for a few basic body functions. Designed for a single doctor and her guests, the Fox River House (1946–1950) had two sleeping areas with double beds and no solid partition between them. It is hard to imagine that this plan would not substantially inhibit social behavior. Mies van der Rohe's "50' x 50'" house, of the same period, has two similarly unseparated sleeping areas, for parents and children.

Steel frame construction. To reflect "honestly" the "truths" of modern construction, many architects felt bound to abandon the interior wall entirely, simply because it was no longer needed to support the building. This was done with little or no understanding of the social function of walls.

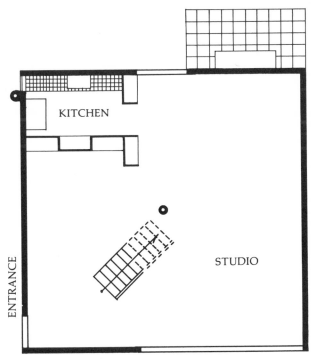

KITCHEN

ENTRANCE

STUDIO

GROUND FLOOR

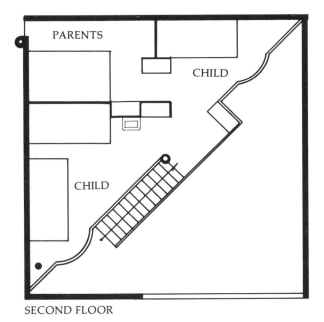

PARENTS

CHILD

CHILD

SECOND FLOOR

Le Corbusier's mass-production dwellings for artisans, designed in 1924, offers another example of the open plan. (Drawings based on plans in Praeger's 1970 edition of *Towards a New Architecture* by Le Corbusier, p. 236)

The effect of these technical innovations on family relationships was ignored because the architect assumed that everyone shared the modern spirit that he had embodied in his open plan. Designers were enchanted with technical potential, and the fact that something could be done at all made it seem desirable to them.

English turned armchair from the sixteenth or seventeenth century. The *Oxford English Dictionary on Historical Principles* says that the word "lathe," in its meaning as a machine for turning wood, came into the English language in the early seventeenth century. This chair could only have been made by someone who was enchanted with the possibilities of the lathe and how it worked. (The Metropolitan Museum of Art. Gift of Mrs. Russel Sage, 1909)

Social Change

A rejection of traditional behavior patterns was implicit in modernists' rejection of traditional architectural forms. However, the past may be dead for the architect, but it lives for others. We know now that there are significant differences between the ways different groups use and perceive their homes, neighborhoods and cities. By denying social continuity, the architect fails to recognize and accommodate these differences in perception. The result is, at best, a lack of economy in planning and, at worst, the development of social pathologies and, finally, physical damage to the buildings.

The phenomenon of change was emphasized to a misleading degree by modernists. To bolster their architectural theories, early modernists had assumed that subcultural differences were disappearing and that industrial societies throughout the world were merging into one homogeneous type. Yet while there had certainly been great changes in the nineteenth century—in urban growth rates for instance—other aspects of society had remained surprisingly constant. But the consistencies were generally overlooked by modernists eager to believe that the past had ceased to be a factor of architectural importance.

The modern rationale for making urban apartments much smaller than traditional city dwellings came largely from the assumption that the average family had become smaller since industrialization; this was, in fact, one of the Bauhaus's main defenses for its housing program. But in one industrial nation, at least, there is contradictory evidence.

In his book *The World We Have Lost*, published in 1965, the English historian Peter Laslett gathered and analyzed information from seventeenth-century English village records and found that large families were the exception in pre-industrial England. He also found that although there certainly were some large households and a large proportion of people lived in large families, the average family was relatively small. He went on to say that more families today have in-laws living with them than was the case in pre-industrial England. Thus the "shrinking family" argument on which the Bauhaus concept of the compact urban apartment was based and which was allegedly valid for all modern industrial cultures is questionable if not inaccurate in the one country for which there are some precise data.

Experts on the cultural perception of space such as Edward T. Hall have shown that even among industrialized societies, cultural differences persist in such apparently universal needs as personal privacy. Iranians have traditionally slept outside, in front of their village houses in the cool, dry summer nights. Today, in westernized Teheran, the descendants and relatives of the villagers still sleep outside, even when their apartments are air-conditioned.

Creating artificial schisms between the past and the present, modernists refused to recognize the value of tradition as a stabilizing factor in human relations, particularly in times of change. Designers were not intersted in *what* had changed, or in the relative value of change versus stability. There was only a broad desire to believe in a grand new age. It was an optimistic age after World War I—the age of communism, nudism and the War to End All Wars.

Iranians have traditionally slept outside in their villages (above),
and many continue to do so in Teheran (below), even though
their apartments may be air-conditioned.

THE NEW HUMANISM

By the early nineteen-fifties a reaction had begun against the inadequacies of the early modern movement's social program. The early modernists had been concerned with how human beings could be better served by architecture, but this concern had focused on the more quantifiable biological requirements rather than on the less specific questions of behavior. Architects produced formulas for determining building spacing to achieve adequate sunshine and fresh air around the buildings, and many studies of the human body to find the best configurations for objects of daily life. But they had not studied or acknowledged the human differences that distinguish separate social groups. The human factor was noticeably missing from their architectural equation.

Although the postwar generation respected the achievements of its predecessors in supplanting historical styles and in revolutionizing the technology of architecture, it was felt that the uniformity and anonymity of early modernism had been the cause of its social failure. Alison and Peter Smithson, founders of the New Brutalist movement in England in the early nineteen-fifties, spoke for the younger architects when they said that the very success of modern architecture meant that we were now "faced with inhuman conditions of a more subtle order than the slums."[24]

The mistake of the early modernists had been to advocate essentially one program for all people in all situations; the technical question had been more important than the social one in determining architectural and planning solutions.

The primary concern of architects now began to shift from the technical aspects of architecture and planning to a more direct accommodation of human needs. One of the first conclusions that architects drew out of this reassessment of social values was that man had to be reidentified with his physical environment. A loosely organized group of European-based architects called Team 10, founded in 1954, was the influential force behind this movement. These architects expressed the feeling that the early modern movement had inadequately dealt with the human element in architecture.

"Expressing" Social Organization in Physical Planning

To reidentify man with his physical environment meant mirroring the social life of the community in its physical structure. Instead of generalized solutions based on technical and mechanical necessities, each social organization—the house, street, district or city—would have its own physical solution, reflecting its own peculiar organization. As the Smithsons pointed out, there is no reason, "for example, for low density family homes to be excluded from the central area of the city, nor is there any need to think conventionally that housing nearer the country should be at lower densities. *It depends on the life pattern of the people who live there what sort of environment is needed* and what sort of density results."[25]

The Smithsons, who were also Team 10 members, were the most articulate exponents of this idea of "expressing" or "mirroring" the social structure in physical form. Actually continuing the earlier anti-historical attitude, they felt that the forms to be expressed were the "new" social forms that had been brought about by the forces of modern times, and that historical forms of house groupings, such as streets, squares and greens, should be abandoned because the social reality they reflected had changed. The architect was to find the right modern symbols to embody the new social realities. Thus, in their project for the Golden Lane housing competition, when observations showed the Smithsons that the social life of the streets was "complex and overlapping," they used a new architectural form that, to them, mirrored these complex relationships without repeating the old form of the street. The chosen form was a series of "streets in the sky" or street decks running along the apartment building at alternating floors that were big enough to hold gatherings of small groups of people without blocking the passage. This arrangement presumably corresponded "more closely to the network of social relationships, as they now exist, than the existing closed patterns of finite spaces and self-contained buildings."[26]

Hard data on the successes of this sort of symbolism are hard to come by, but in 1961, the town of Sheffield, England, built Park Hill, a housing project that consists of one continuous building, varying in height from three to fourteen stories and using essentially the same idea of street decks as the Smithsons' Golden Lane project. The apartments were entered from an exterior corridor located at every third floor that ran the full length of the meandering building and was wide enough—12 feet—to allow for large gatherings of people without blocking the corridor. It even permitted such traditional ground-level street activities as milk deliveries by small vans. The street decks seemed like an ideal marriage of traditional ways of life and new architectural forms. Some six years after the first residents had moved in, a social worker and resident of Park Hill took a random one-in-five sample survey of tenants to get their reactions to the project. The survey, which was published in *Architectural Review* in 1967, showed that, as a means of access, the decks were very successful. One third of the people liked the fact that the decks were "dry" or "sheltered," and about 10 percent appreciated being able to walk the full length of the project without having to go down and then up again. But the decks seem to have had little effect as generators of social activities compared to the streets they were supposed to have replaced. Only 4 percent of the people "remembered" that they could use the decks as a place in which to stand and talk with their friends.

While it is undoubtedly good to recognize that social relationships within a community are complex and overlapping rather than simple and direct, there is not necessarily a direct relationship between complex physical geometry and complexity of social intercourse. The rich social life in the simplest gridiron city suffices to show that social and physical complexity are independent of one another.

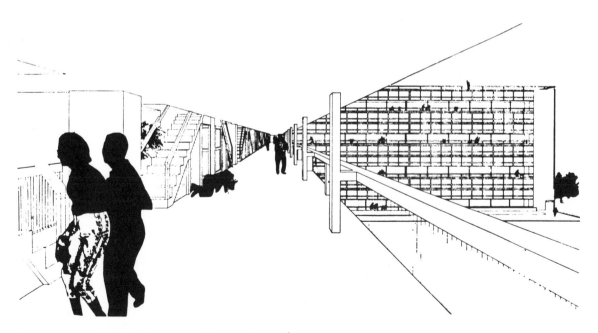

Submission for the 1952 Golden Lane Housing Project, by Alison and Peter Smithson, showing the "street in the sky." (From *Urban Structuring* by Alison and Peter Smithson)

Assuming for the moment that behavior patterns could be "expressed" or "mirrored" in the environment, to be successful the forms that "mirror" the pattern must be immediately comprehensible. Some expressions of experiences are easily comprehended—such as the sensation of movement, which is familiar to everyone. We recognize the symbols of motion in Boccioni's statue *Unique Forms of Continuity in Space* because we associate them with our own common experience: the angle of the limbs, the tilt of the torso and even the flaps are reminiscent of windblown hair or clothing. We see the statue as a symbol of movement because of these associations.

Proper understanding of people's behavior patterns requires having shared their experience, either by living in the situation or through carefully structured study. When people do not have the same associations, they often fail to perceive correctly. Early locomotives moved at much greater speeds than people were accustomed to, and because they had no similar experience to relate it to, some people felt that the locomotive speeding toward them was not an object of constant size moving closer, but a stationary object that kept getting larger. In one case, during the opening of the Liverpool and Manchester railroad in England in 1830, the misperception resulted in the death of an overcurious onlooker.

Above, the anthropomorphic figure of Boccioni's *Unique Forms of Continuity in Space* conveys a sense of movement because we associate its forms with our own experience of movement—for example, the windblown hair in the photograph below. (Umberto Boccioni's sculpture—1913, bronze, 43⅞ x 34⅞ x 15¾". Collection, The Museum of Modern Art, New York. Acquired through the Lillie P. Bliss Bequest)

If the physical expression of the social pattern is to be understood by the designer and the user, there must be some common ground between them. The problem is that when the user is from a different culture or class than the architect, there are often fewer shared social experiences, and when designers refuse to look at how people actually live and instead establish their own patterns, the lack of common ground is assured.

Officers' Club in Ta'iz, Yemen, 1971. This photo is taken from one of the main entertainment rooms and shows the view through an archway to the rest room. There is no door shielding the rest room from the club room. The probable explanation is that women, most of whom are in purdah in Yemen, would never be entertained in the club.

It is beginning to be accepted that the designer must familiarize himself with the user's living patterns. For example, a street that cannot be seen from the home may be considered an acceptable children's playground for some lower economic classes because the parents do not mind if their children are informally supervised by older children or other adults. Middle-class parents, however, feel they must supervise their children directly and would probably consider the unobserved street dangerous. To each group the unobserved street means something different and therefore each will use it differently. If the architect is unaware of the differences, his design may have nothing to do with the way the people are actually going to use it.

Middle-class mothers seldom let their younger children walk the city streets alone; they accompany them to playgrounds and closely supervise them.

Whether from choice or necessity, these Black children are given the responsibility of taking care of their younger brothers and sisters.

Above, symbolic front porch furniture made of cast iron. The real visiting and relaxing is done behind the house in the middle-class suburb, as shown below.

This porch in a working-class district in Spartanburg, South Carolina, has furniture that is used for serious sitting.

Failure or success in accommodating behavior patterns depends on two factors: how specific the social information is and how sensitively the architect translates this specific information into physical form. Assume, for instance, that observations have shown that the following conditions exist:

1. There are frequent contacts between neighbors in the same building.
2. People rely heavily on their neighbors for help and comfort during times of stress.
3. The concept of "neighborliness" is a highly prized commodity among members of the community.

These observations allow us to suggest specific design solutions, one solution would be to place the apartment entrances close together, making it easy to continue the pattern of neighborliness. The contact between neighbors would undoubtedly also continue if the entrances were put at opposite ends of the hallway, but this would introduce an unnecessary strain.

The main point is that generalized social concepts are useless. They are so vague that one is not sure design decisions based on them will affect behavior positively, negatively or not at all.

The Smithsons took the observation that urban social life was complex and tried to encourage this pattern by paralleling the complex social structure with a complex physical structure. They were fooled by the fact that the original observation was too general. One of the smaller facets of this generalization is that the complex behavior they spoke of required a certain density in order to take place, and by multiplying the possible places to meet, they diffused the people and activities and therefore reduced the frequency of contact. The people of Sheffield apparently reacted by not using the street decks for meeting their friends. Because the observation was too general, it did not indicate any specific requirements. Because there were no specific design requirements, the architects could revert to a poetic formal interpretation of the idea of "complex social structure."

More specific information could have led to a more effective solution. Had the architects found, for example, that the laundromat or the butcher shop was an important place for social interaction, or that community news was informally disseminated from the pub, they might have been able to reinforce social intercourse by careful placement of these services.

Another example of social information that is too general is the presumption that the hearth as the center of home life is a concept common to all cultures and therefore a bona fide generator of design decisions.

It may be true that all dwellings have hearths, or centers of family life, but this says nothing about the necessary relationships between the hearth and other parts of the house that certainly vary from group to group. Only when the architect has specific information about how living patterns affect these relationships can he use the general observation that the hearth is a special place.

In a study for apartment renovation in Puerto Rican Harlem, the firm of Brolin/Zeisel found that the kitchen was the center of family life—interesting information but not helpful in locating the kitchen in the apartment plan. Another observation was more helpful: the woman, who spends much of the day in the kitchen, must be able to monitor who comes and goes from the apartment. This specific information could be translated into a specific design inference: a person in the kitchen must be able to see the apartment entrance. This could be accomplished electronically, but the budget ruled this out. Therefore the kitchen had to be close to the entrance. With more information—should the sleeping areas be private; should people who come to the entrance be able to see into the living areas; should eating and entertaining areas be separated—the architect was able to locate the kitchen more precisely.

Although not all behavior patterns can or should be accommodated in design, the architect must know about the patterns so that his design does not obstruct them. In many working-class families, the woman is more in charge of running the household than the man. She takes care of the children, cooks, cleans, shops and even looks for a new apartment when necessary. Yet, to try to express this symbolically, by subordinating all other spaces of the apartment to the kitchen, for example, could infringe on another requirement, the respect for the man as breadwinner and titular head of the family.

ORIGINAL TENEMENT PLAN

EAST 110 STREET

REVISED PLAN

EAST 110 STREET

This rehabilitation of an old-law tenement in Puerto Rican Harlem, New York City, was based on the following requirements as defined by observational and interview research:

1. *Observation:* Women spend the majority of their time in the kitchen during the day.
   Observation: Women want to keep close tabs on their children and on anyone else who might come or go from the apartment
   Observation: Doors from living rooms to public hall are not used because of a need to keep tabs on children and because the living room is a "sacred space" for special occasions.
   Requirement: The kitchen must serve as a lock to monitor the apartment entrance. Entrance should not be directly into the living room.

2. *Observation:* Peer groups prefer to separate in the evenings in order to socialize.
   Requirement: Two separate spaces large enough to accommodate small groups. Connections should be minimal.

Proximity Breeds Relationships

Trying to increase social contacts by providing many potential meeting places, as the Smithsons did with their streets in the sky, is a variation on the idea that proximity breeds relationships. According to this notion the more opportunities there are to meet, the more actual meetings will take place. At least one building seems to contradict this theory and to support the old proverb that good fences make good neighbors: the Yale Art and Architecture Building designed by architect Paul Rudolph in 1963 that houses the schools of architecture, planning and fine arts.

The various departments were put together in one building to encourage communication among the different faculties and student bodies. At the main entrance and on each floor there are large elevator lobbies and hallways designed to encourage lingering, and, in addition, a coffee house was created on the top floor that was well-patronized by all departments. Yet, to a student who knew the architecture school both before and after the construction of the A & A Building, interdepartmental communication did not noticeably increase because of the proximity.

In some situations, proximity actually reduced the probability of communication, as in the case of painters' studios located on the top floor. The elevator lobby on this floor, which also housed the vending machines, provided the only access to the coffee shop in the penthouse. There was considerable traffic through the area and, inevitably, curiosity led some people into the warren of painters' cubicles just off the lobby. Good for communication, one might think, but in a short time the painters had raised makeshift barricades and eventually they requested and received a permanent lockable door to seal themselves off.

The coffee shop was the subject of continual studies by the "use-oriented" architecture students. It was convenient, heavily trafficked and seemed a natural place for social mixing. However, from my observations, I would say it was used less to strike up new acquaintances than to meet already established friends. The new connections among students seemed to come more through "forced" propinquity—being in the same class or having to find someone with whom to share an apartment—than from casual meetings in the coffee shop.

New Forms Reflecting "New" Social Patterns

Although second-generation modernists, and most notably members of Team 10, reacted against the social programs of the first-generation architects, they continued the idea that the present-day architecture needed totally new forms in order to express the new, modern way of life. The Smithsons used the physical mobility of modern life as the generator of this "new" physical form.

The average worker no longer lived where he worked, they reasoned, but commuted to administrative or industrial areas from outlying residential areas. In their "Cluster City," they grouped residential, office, factory and ceremonial quarters in separate clusters that were connected by highly articulated "urban motorways" and secondary local roads. In their eyes, this created a new physical image reflecting the new social reality. Actually, the bedroom suburb had already existed for sixty or seventy years. The innovation of Cluster City, then, was a new *simplified graphic form*

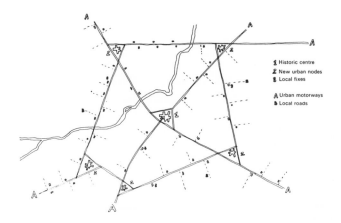

Alison and Peter Smithsons' Cluster City, ca. 1956.

of what already existed rather than the creation of a new form for living. Bearing this in mind, one can see that the incorporation of social patterns becomes less significant than the new graphic form itself. The Smithsons themselves stressed that what they were presenting was above all an "image," "a new aesthetic."[27] Cluster City is less an attempt to formalize new social patterns than it is another chapter in the modern movement's search for an image of the times. The social aspect is used as a device to justify what is felt to be an innovative form in much the same way that the early modernists used new technical capabilities to justify their new forms.

New Forms and Persisting Social Patterns

In 1947, the Atelier de Batisseurs (ATBAT) was formed by Le Corbusier. In 1955, three of ATBAT's members—Bodiansky, Candilis and Woods—designed housing for Morocco, paying special attention to one aspect of traditional Muslim life, the preeminence of the patio as a completely private meeting place for the family. The traditional courtyard was reworked into a patio that retained at least one of the attributes of the original court, its privacy from the outside. The building, of course, was designed in the modern style. The inclusion of the traditional patio element in an otherwise modern form was a sensitive choice and a major break with the idea that everyone ought to share the architect's values. Although this fact alone sets the building apart from its predecessors, the question must still be raised: Why is the new form needed if the same traditions persist?

Since the ATBAT building seems to stand in a large open space, it is doubtful that land conservation was the reason for this "high-rise" patio apartment house. Surely the answer lies in the modernist's compulsion to break with visual tradition, whether or not there is a practical reason for doing so. The building plan acknowledges the importance of a social tradition, but its multi-level form and modern elevation deny the importance of visual traditions. This kind of schizophrenic division of social versus visual needs is typical of recent generations of modernists concerned with "humanizing" modern architecture. In fact, a government housing project built at the same time in the traditional Moroccan style is referred to by the architects as "perhaps no solution at all, culturally speaking."[28] With this verbal sleight-of-hand the continuing visual culture of Morocco, manifested in the traditional form of the dwelling, is summarily dismissed in favor of the international visual language of modern architecture. Modern architects' faith in the modern age is so strong that, for them, the very modernity of the vertical apartment living assures its correctness, while the traditional style of the government housing automatically condemns it.

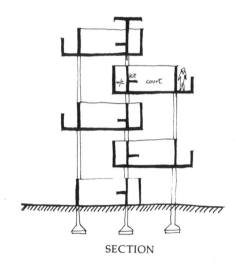

SECTION

PLAN

Collective housing in Morocco by Bodiansky, Candilis and Woods. The section and plan show the incorporation of the traditional private court of Moroccan houses. (After drawing in *Architectural Design*, January 1955, p. 2)

Persistence of Social Traditions

Second-generation modernists reemphasized the earlier modern viewpoint that the social life of contemporary man is so radically different from the past that it cannot possibly be accommodated in the same physical containers of traditional streets, houses and other forms. But glancing around quickly tells us that, if anything, the opposite is true: no matter what culture it is used in, the greatest social distress seems to be caused by the high-rise, and this is the only new housing form of the century. Meanwhile, many people, including architects, buy and renovate nineteenth-century town houses.

A look at the Italian communities in the United States shows that behavior patterns of third and fourth generation Italian-Americans parallel the life styles of urban and village dwellers in Italy. The most obvious similarity is in the use of the street as an outdoor living room.

The piazza as a meeting place in Aosta, Italy.

The street as a meeting place in Little Italy, New York City.

Another supposed anachronism is the suburban single-family tract house, considered by most architects to be culturally obsolete. By all standards, however, it remains the most popular form of housing in this country. Architects are really expressing their condemnation of the social and aesthetic values that it represents when they claim that it is anachronistic.

Of necessity the suburb demands an inhibiting regularity. Each house must have a lot of approximately the same size, for economic reasons. Because the client wants a free-standing house, it must be put pretty much in the same place: the middle of that lot.

Most of the possible variations have been tried already, and "originality" in the cherished modern sense of demonstrating the designer's individuality is virtually impossible. The houses are spread evenly over the land, with no accents, no variation and no subtle patterns or contrasts, or at least none that the architect can discern. Yet for the owners there is enough difference in the slight variations of color, trim or lot placement.

Nineteenth- and early twentieth-centry homes in Haverstraw, New York. The single-family home has been preferred in the United States even when, as here, its separateness has been more symbolic than real.

Furthermore, the average suburbanite is likely to be more conservative than the architect. He is probably anti-intellectual, pro-tradition and generally conformist, whereas the architect often sees himself at the leading edge of cultural change. Fortunately or unfortunately, suburbs depress architects more than they depress the people who live in them.

Suburbia's regularity has made it an anathema to architects.

The suburban regularity that architects perceive is at the larger scale, which means little to the suburbanite. The small additions he makes to his home, such as these carriage lamps, are enough for him.

Flexibility and User-Participation

In the past decade there have been an increasing number of projects using flexibility as a means of personalizing architecture and accommodating different life styles. This principle offers the user the possibility of changing, or making some individual contribution to, his own house. Proposals incorporating flexibility are not new; in 1919 Adolph Loos suggested a changeable scheme for workers' housing, and examples of flexible housing exist as early at least as the mid-nineteenth-century.

Flexibility can help to accommodate varying social needs. In using the tenant's participation, it may also make him feel that he has more at stake, and consequently he may take better care of the property. One way to include flexibility in housing was through the "open aesthetic," which was formulated by Team 10 at Otterloo, in 1959 and should not be confused with the open plan of early modern architecture. The open aesthetic was the architectural equivalent of a "happening," an artistic event of that time in which the process was as important as the product. It offered the user the possibility to change or add to the completed house so that inhabitants could mark their housing with their own individual stamp.

The open aesthetic was a still more extreme move away from the early, impersonal modern architecture since it allowed the user to make changes to suit his own needs and was an improvement over the idea of visually symbolizing social behavior. Helping to build one's own house, even on the small scale of participating in semi-skilled construction work, is an excellent way to begin bringing the house and the way people use it closer together. Obviously, the more the client is involved in the basic planning decisions, such as determining room sizes and locations, the better the idea works, but unfortunately, the more one tends toward this specific an involvement of the client, the more cumbersome the process becomes.

However, there are successful examples of this approach in different parts of the world. The owner-planned squatter settlements around many South American towns are the most extreme and most publicized examples. In these, a professional is seldom involved at all; everything is owner-planned, from the initial occupation of the free land to the construction of individual houses. Although these settlements began illegally, their subsequent success in establishing a working community and solving housing problems with a minimum of public expense and social stress have led to government approval in the form of aid.

Mass-produced housing in 1853. (Courtesy Art and Architecture Division, of The New York Public Library. Astor, Tilden and Lenox Foundations)

HOUSE DURING TRANSPORTATION.

Such planned or unplanned do-it-yourself housing costs less than architect-designed housing. Self-help means lower construction cost and the materials are usually locally available. The problem with foreign architects in developing countries is that they often are not familiar with local materials or they feel that such materials are inappropriate to modern times. Consequently they import more expensive and sophisticated materials and, with them, costly machinery and technical skills. Another seldom recognized advantage of using local materials is that the money spent for them is fed back into the local economy.

In the early nineteen-sixties the objections to urban renewal were beginning to be expressed. It became evident that many of the mistakes of urban renewal had happened because there was no contact between policy-makers and those who were eventually affected by the policies. In the wake of its failure, lay groups are learning the legal, financial and architectural skills necessary to co-op and rehabilitate the buildings in their own neighborhoods for considerably less than what new buildings would cost.

Communities threatened by official planning proposals often have the services of a professional who acts as an advocate for their cause. The professional helps formulate the community's needs and desires so that the inhabitants can offer articulate and knowledgeable alternatives to those of the official agency. The value of such proceedings for establishing community spirit is obvious. The community has the services of a professional, yet it can determine its own priorities.

Mega-structures would seem to offer the ultimate in flexibility for accommodating different social needs. They usually consist of huge structural frameworks, varying in size from a few stories to several thousand feet high, into which individual room-size or apartment-size units can be put in or taken out at will. Thus, when the family grows, it buys another room unit and adds it on; when the children marry and leave, the couple sells the extra space and goes back to the pre-children apartment size. The ease of changing is possible because the units are mass-produced, interchangeable and independent of the supporting structure and services. But forgetting for a moment the complications of moving large apartment-sized objects through dense urban areas, it seems that mega-structures would only be flexible if they were not used to capacity, and therefore were uneconomical. With a profitable 3, or even 5, percent vacancy rate a mega-structure becomes relatively inflexible: you cannot expand

Often, imported materials are defeated by the rigors of climate that traditional materials have withstood for centuries. In the Russian school in Sanaa, Yemen, a concrete building, recently built, shows severe cracking due to extreme temperature changes.

if your neighbor will not contract.

There are other complications in using flexible structures that grow or shrink as the family's needs change, or that can be junked when they go out of style, like the family car. Technology does not become obsolete as fast as the worshipers of change would have us believe. The disposable units may last too long and become too valuable to throw away. Planners may have confused the rate of social change and technological obsolescence with the speed of communication that is now possible. Jet-age travel was ushered in in the late nineteen-fifties by airplanes that are still flying fifteen years later and that will probably still be used another fifteen years from now. This thirty-year period covers the life of a normal home mortgage.

Many of the flexible units proposed for mass housing draw on aero-space technology and, with maintenance, will certainly last as long as the Boeing 707. If they do last thirty years, and go through several owners, perhaps we should not ask how we can make a movable architecture but continue asking whether, when a new apartment is needed, it is not easier to move the people and their belongings rather than the apartment.

Smaller-scale ways of achieving flexibility, like movable interior walls, are not much more flexible than the mega-structure in practice. A young couple needing a one-bedroom apartment now but a nursery in two years must rent enough space for the nursery from the beginning. Otherwise they must take away from the existing space to get the extra room when they need it.

In rental space, where economy rather than prestige is important, partitions are seldom more flexible than a four-inch concrete block wall. A tenant with a three-year lease needs no more flexibility than that. Even in museums, which change their exhibits as often as every six weeks, stud walls with plasterboard are sufficiently flexible.

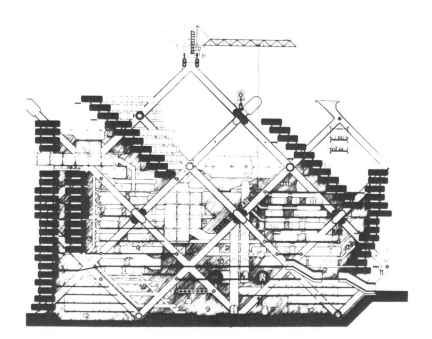

Section through architect Peter Cook's Plug-in City, designed in 1964, showing a dual level highway at the upper right and a crane for plugging in and unplugging individual units.

The extent to which there is a demand for changeable walls is also moot. Most nonarchitects have neither the interest nor the inclination to move walls in their homes. When one considers the complex technology needed to create and maintain these flexible environments and weighs that against the number of times they would actually be "flexed," one is left with an obvious case of overkill.

A defiant example that form does not determine behavior and that "mobility" and "immobility" are relative terms: The two houses in the photograph below are on wheels, being moved through the Virginia countryside. The "mobile home" above has been permanently entrenched along the Hudson River.

If flexibility were to be a useful way to accommodate different ways of life, we would have to be careful who defined its boundaries. One range of flexibility may be proper for one group and wrong for another, and if the architect establishes the range around his own norm and it does not coincide with that of his clients, the whole concept is invalidated. A door, for example, offers a considerable range of flexibility for determining the relationship between two spaces. At different times during the day we open it, close it or set it at any one of an infinite number of gradations between those two limits. We might assume that this would be flexibility enough to suit the needs of any culture. Yet we would be as wrong as the Europeans and European-trained Indian architects who, when they designed the houses in Chandigarh, assumed that the European range of flexibility offered by the door would be necessary to satisfy all needs; in fact it proved to be irrelevant. The majority of interior doors that the author saw in the homes of Chandigarh were unused. Questioning disclosed that they were kept fully open, even bedroom doors at night, and curtains were hung over the openings instead.

Regardless of mobility or immobility, the architect must recognize the importance of symbolism. Note the mullioned window and arched doorway sewn into this canvas trailer porch in Italy. The door opens by zipper.

IV.

Two Case Studies in the Application of the Modern Ideology

CHANDIGARH, INDIA

As we have seen, the modern ideology is a statement about how people should live and how the containers in which they live should look. One of the basic beliefs held by modernists was that this ideology was universally relevant to the modern industrial world because it advocated rational planning to meet the unique circumstances of modern life.

Whether in designing a house or a city, the concept of planning presumes one's ability to predict how the plan will be used. The closer the planner's intentions are realized in actual use, the more successful his design premises have been. If the people for whom the house, or city, was planned do not use it in the way the planner predicted, the planner and the plan have failed. Obviously there are degrees of success and it is impossible to be right all the time, but if the architect designs one room specifically as a living room and another as a bedroom, and the occupants sleep in the living room and entertain their guests in the bedroom, he should not boast about the remarkable adaptability of his plan. He has failed to see and accommodate people's needs.

Finally, if the modern ideology is to be successful, the planning alternatives it proposes— how it wants people to live—must prove more durable and desirable than the traditions it seeks to replace. When this happens, the modernists will have proven their point and we need never again consider tradition a factor in architecture.

Chandigarh, capital of the Punjab and Hariana provinces of India, was designed and planned according to the modern Western principles that have been discussed in this book. It offered a unique chance to test the validity of the modernists' theories because of the circumstances of its planning and growth over the past twenty years. Chandigarh was designed and built on a virgin site, so that there were no preexisting traditional forms to hinder the relatively pure application of modern architectural and planning concepts.

There were, of course, technical and economic restrictions, but one can hardly have a fair test of any theory without them. Basically, Le Corbusier and his associates had as free a hand in the planning and execution of Chandigarh as any architect in the West could hope for. Thus the success or failure of Chandigarh comes as close as possible to being a reasonable test application for modern theories.

Construction was begun in 1952, and when I visited the site in 1971, all major elements of the first phase had been completed and the second phase had begun.

Chandigarh's population is composed mainly of government workers who are better educated and more "Westernized" than the populations of other Indian cities. The city was conceived in the afterglow of India's independence, when Prime Minister Nehru wanted to lead Indians away from both their colonial past and their Indian traditions. The circumstances could hardly have been more auspicious for the modernist, anxious to prove the homogenization of the world's peoples. In this section I will look at this Western designed Indian city from the point of view of how well the intended uses have been realized over the past twenty years, without intending a specific criticism of Le Corbusier or of the Indian and European professionals who have worked on the planning of the city over the past two decades. Chandigarh is the product of a state of mind that continues to manifest itself in many large and small projects all over the world, and the discussion should be considered in this larger context.

The old Punjab capital of Lahore, which was lost to Pakistan when India was partitioned in 1947, had been the cultural, educational and political center of Northern India, and its loss was severely felt. To boost the spirits of the people, to make them feel they had not lost everything, Prime Minister Nehru chose to build a new city for the capital rather than enlarge one of the existing provincial cities. In his words, the new city should be "unfettered by traditions."

After several false starts the Indian government settled on Le Corbusier as the chief architect and planner, and in March and April of 1950 he visited Punjab. The realized city lies on a plain, in view of the Himalayan foothills. The first phase consists of thirty sectors, each a half mile wide by three quarters of a mile long, divided by a grid of major traffic arteries. The building height in this phase was limited to two and a half stories; the city was to have taller buildings in the second phase. Special sectors are devoted specifically to industry and the university, but the typical sector consists of housing, a local shopping center and local schools, temples and other community buildings.

Plan of Chandigarh. Phase one. (Courtesy of Burma-Shell)

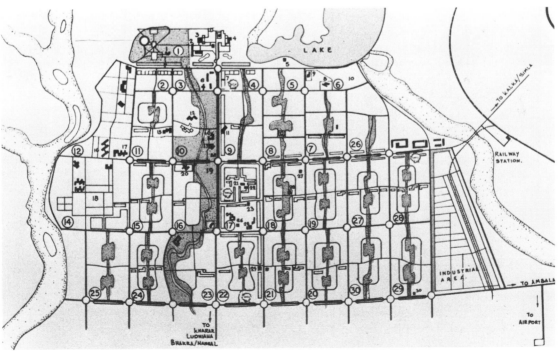

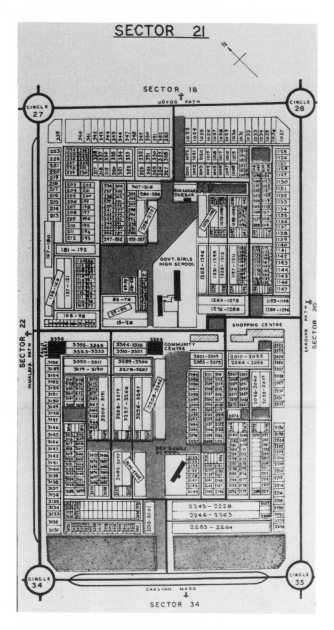

SECTOR 21

A residential sector in Chandigarh. (Courtesy of Burma-Shell)

The typical residential sector has two places where cars can enter on an east-west commercial street, and this street has smaller roads leading from it to the housing areas. The main business center is in the center of the city, Sector 17, while the government buildings, the only ones designed by Le Corbusier, are located to the north near a man-made lake, which was formed by damming a seasonal river that used to run through the site. The land on both sides of this riverbed, now called Leisure Valley, is the city's major park.

Open Spaces

The demand for open space, fresh air and light, which as we have seen was an important requirement of the modern movement, played a decisive role in Chandigarh's planning and, ironically, is responsible for its present distinctly suburban character. There are three different scales of open space in the city:

1. The city-wide park called Leisure Valley; 2. major parks that run north–south through each residential sector; and 3. the smaller open spaces around houses.

Leisure Valley extends from the north to south through the entire first planning phase and was meant to be a focal point of activity for the city's residents. To Westerners, the idea of a city-wide park is familiar; we are all acquainted with the large parks in most major European and American cities. Yet compared to its Western counterparts, Leisure Valley is little used. The problem arising here applies to nearly all aspects of Chandigarh's physical planning: the designers made assumptions about how people were going to use the city without taking into account the traditional Indian way of life.

90

Leisure Valley.

Park sitters in Washington Square, New York City.

The Taj Mahal. (1630–1652)

Time and again we talked with residents who told us that the parks were foreigners' inventions. Of course, there are beautiful parks in India, but they are, by and large, imports. The Taj Mahal and its grounds were built during the Moghul occupation and the parks of New Delhi during the British occupation. In general Indians are family-oriented to a far greater extent than most Europeans and their recreaton and entertainment take place in the home. Whereas an American family would go the park for a weekend outing, its Indian counterpart would be more likely to visit the home of a family member. A Western mother automatically takes her child to the park to play, but an Indian woman might easily be accused of improprieties if she appeared in a public park unescorted by her husband. In some parts of India the English-speaking, educated hostess will not hand a man a cup of tea for fear their hands might touch and people begin to talk.

The green spaces within the sectors, particularly those around the shopping centers and offices, are more appreciated than Leisure Valley. These spaces correspond to spaces which are used in traditional Indian towns and villages. Even in villages men will gather under the shade of a tree to talk or play cards, and in all cities men gather in friends' shops or on the street to talk with friends. However, although the spaces around the sector shopping centers do permit this traditional behavior to continue, they are usually so large that they destroy the feeling of urban life that is characteristic of other Indian cities.

The great size of these spaces also gives rise to unintended uses. They are intended as buffers between commercial and residential areas, but often they are also illegally usurped by shopkeepers and used as warehouses or extra factory space.

Following the traditional Indian pattern, green spaces outside
offices are well used during lunch hours.

Spaces between shopping centers and housing are often taken
over illegally by shop owners or manufacturers.

The green spaces around houses are probably the most successful because they follow the traditional pattern most closely. Indian women generally stay close to home and their children also play nearby. Yet even in this relatively successful area of the plan, there are problems that could have been easily avoided had the designers realized the durability of traditions. The *mulhalla*, the traditional Indian urban residential street, is relatively narrow, sometimes as little as four or five feet across, with the houses ranging from one to four or five stories high. Particularly among the lower classes, the custom is for the women to sit in front of their houses, talking among themselves and doing their daily chores. In Chandigarh the low-income houses are often grouped around squares as much as eighty or a hundred feet across. People still sit in front of their houses around the periphery, but the central space (the Westerner would call it the piazza or green) is a no-man's land. Whereas in an analogous working-class community in the West the space would have become the focal point of the neighborhood, in India the family area is more important.

The traditional residential street in an Indian city, the *mulhalla*.

Neighborhood Unit

Of Chandigarh's thirty sectors, approximately twenty-five are primarily residential and based on the neighborhood unit idea. This planning concept has been popular in the West for over forty years and is ultimately traceable as far back as the nineteenth-century suburban "superblock." Gropius defined the neighborhood units as areas "small enough to serve as organisms for reactivating social intercourse."[29]

One of the purposes of the neighborhood unit, or "sector" as it is called in Chandigarh, is to break the population down into small cells that can form closely knit communities. The theory behind the neighborhood idea is that it will encourage community feeling because people are grouped relatively close together in an identifiable area, with one elementary school for all children and all residents using the same conveniently located parks and shopping centers. The growth of community feeling is supposed to be aided by the fact that these people all come from approximately the same economic class.

The neighborhood concept has been successful in this country, but the assumptions that made it successful here have proven inappropriate in the Indian context. In the United States, before bussing, parents who wanted their children to attend public schools were required to send them to the school in their district. In addition, parents normally participated in local Parent-Teacher Association meetings and voted in the local board of education elections. All of these factors made the school a focus for the community, a point of common interest around which people could rally.

By our standards there is a proliferation of schools in India, and public schools do not form the basis of the educational system. Children are sent to any of many different private schools depending upon, we were told, the family's social status, religious beliefs, and/or economic status. Thus, the elementary school is not the nucleus of the community. In some instances, according to a study done in the Punjab University Sociology Department, 98 percent of the schoolchildren in a given sector went to school outside that sector.

Courtyard in the low-income housing of Chandigarh.

People in this country who buy houses costing approximately the same amount have something else in common on which to build a sense of community: they earn about the same amount of money. Although in Chandigarh the residents of each sector are of virtually the same economic class (since they have been grouped according to government housing classifications), this is evidently not a catalyst for neighborliness. Family ties were by far the most important single factor in forming friendships among the people we talked with and observed.

Houses of the same class are grouped together in a Chandigarh sector.

In theory, the commercial focus of the sector was another way of providing community feeling. The sector shopping centers were to have several stores of different kinds so that people would not have to go outside the sector for the daily necessities. Here again, custom foiled the planners' intentions. In the traditional bazaar, which the new shopping centers were to replace, shops selling similar goods group together. The one-of-each-kind-of-shop shopping center in Chandigarh was destined for trouble from the beginning, and trouble has come in several ways. Most noticeably, several shopping centers have been taken over by one type of store alone. There is one that has only auto and motorcycle repair shops, another with only furniture and still another with all construction-related goods. When this happens, the necessities of life for that particular sector are provided by illegal vendors who set up their semi-permanent carts in the park spaces around the shopping centers. (Cart vendors are allowed in the city, but only if they keep moving.) The planners are disturbed because these conglomerations of vendors are extremely untidy and are, of course, blatantly ignoring the law.

The reasons for this invasion of illegal merchants are not completely clear. Surely at some point in the past, and perhaps even now, grouping similar shops together made it easier for people who could not read to find things. Another possibility is that shopping in India, as well as in many other parts of the world, is not the simple, impersonal act it has come to be for us in the West, where we walk down endless aisles, pick what we want from shelves and never see a clerk until we go to the cashier. In India the process is much more colorful and demands more human contact. Bargaining is an important part of it and is facilitated by grouping shops selling similar goods in one location. This makes it easy for the buyer to get prices from different shops and for the seller to keep tabs on his competition.

Some of the sector shopping centers that were originally meant
to have a variety of shops now have only one kind of shop.

When the official shopping centers have only one kind of shop,
illegal vendors establish semipermanent stalls to provide the
other necessities of daily life.

In the shopping centers where the permanent buildings have not been occupied exclusively by one kind of store, illegal vendors have moved in and provide alternatives for shoppers who would otherwise be limited to only one merchant for each type of merchandise. Thus while there may be only one or two shops of the same kind in the official center, there may be twenty illegal vendors camped out in the mall selling the same goods.

Despite by-laws and zoning restrictions limiting commercial development to the shopping areas, a huge illegal bazaar covering several acres has grown up in Sector 23. Here the vendors have grouped themselves traditionally according to the type of goods sold.

The shopping centers were planned for only one side of the main east-west street in each sector in order to limit the number of pedestrians disrupting traffic by crossing the street to go from one store to another. Yet although the streets seem inhibitingly wide, the houses opposite the official shops have almost all been converted to commercial uses. The traditional street form of the bazaar, though devitalized by attenuation, still survives.

The main streets of the residential sectors were planned with shops on only the south (right) side. In every case, however, the traditional Indian commercial form, the bazaar street, has been realized and the houses across from the shopping center have become shops.

Housing

The remarks in this section pertain only to the thirteen types of government houses that were designed by or under the supervision of the original planners, and not to the many privately designed houses. We observed and talked with residents of all thirteen types and the following paragraphs cover some of the problems that we observed or that were mentioned to us.

By and large, the richer the resident, the more likely he was to be either satisfied with the basic layout of the house or aware that Chandigarh had been designed by an important person and, with the Indian deference to authority, feel that he should be respectful. For instance the occupants of the house that will be described in detail next had no complaints about their house, even though they had had to redesign it in order to live the way they wanted to. Their expression of satisfaction was predictable to some extent because they were government employees and they did not want to bite the hand that fed them. In another, more important sense, Chandigarh offered some basic amenities that we take for granted but that are rare in India. Perhaps the single most praised feature of the city was its closed sewer system and flush-system toilets.

The floor plan of the house shown in the accompanying illustration is simple: entry into a living room and passage straight through past the kitchen on the left and two connected bedrooms on the right to a rear verandah. The water closet is in a small room on the verandah, separated from the rest of the house in a way that suits the traditional Indian desire for cleanliness. Upon examination we saw that only two rooms were used entirely as intended—one of the bedrooms and the verandah with the water closet.

The Indian home is private. When someone who is not a member of the extended family enters, the family's privacy must be protected, and therefore the room where the guest is entertained, referred to as the drawing room, must be visually separated from the family areas. In this house plan, the family areas comprise the kitchen, bedrooms, rear verandah, courtyard and bathroom—what would have been the woman's areas in the traditional Indian home. Originally, the occupants of this house found that the drawing room was too open in relation to the rest of the house. To remedy this, they shifted its functions to the front bedroom and boarded up the connecting door to the other bedroom. The guest is still brought through the intended drawing room, but once in the new drawing room the curtain can be drawn and the family can go discreetly about its business. Had they owned the house, this Indian family confided, they would have blocked up the original entry, and made a door into the front bedroom.

The intended living room has become the second bedroom, where the grandfather and the thirteen-year-old son sleep in one large bed. The second bedroom is occupied by the man, his wife and their eleven-year-old daughter in one bed, and the year-old baby beside them on a mat.

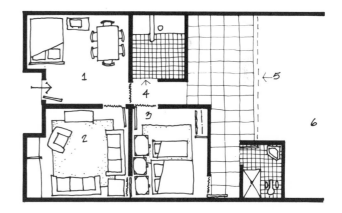

Floor plan for a house in Chandigarh.
1. Was living/dining room; now bedroom/dining room.
2. Was bedroom; now drawing room.
3. Bedroom with box storage and closet as shrine.
4. Kitchen with counter-top stove.
5. Rear verandah and work area.
6. Enclosed rear courtyard.

There was no closeable niche provided for the family altar, so the closet has been taken over for this and clothes hung on pegs in the wall or stored in boxes stacked around the room.

The small kitchen was intended only for cooking, but tradition persists and the family also eats there. Unfortunately, the kitchen's size prevents them from eating together and they must eat in shifts. One thing that should be mentioned here is that the staple bread of India, the chapati, must be eaten immediately after it is cooked. Without servants, it is impossible for the woman to participate in the meal and still serve freshly cooked chapatis unless the family eats in the kitchen.

A stand-up counter was built into the kitchen to hold the kerosene stove, but, in general, these counters are not used. The wife cooks on the floor—which is kept scrupulously clean—and the family eats from plates put on the floor. In more Westernized houses there are dining tables and chairs, although the rather sensible tradition of eating without knives and forks continues. Upon questioning we were generally told that the tables were used primarily when guests came whom it was important to impress.

The Indian concept of privacy is puzzling to a Westerner. For example, a high Indian planning official living in one of the larger Western-designed houses has three generous bedrooms at his family's disposal, but he and his wife sleep in one and their four teen-age children—two boys and two girls—in another, while the third is vacant This is very difficult to understand if you come from a culture where a child often has his own bedroom before he is out of the cradle.

Lacking a place for the family shrine, the Indian family used the closet.

A number of factors in Chandigarh's planning testify to the architects' misunderstanding of the Indian sense of privacy. In a number of cases where fashionably modern floor-to-ceiling windows were used, they have been papered over by the houses' occupants. The living room, and particularly the bedroom, are private sanctums and the possibility of strangers seeing through a window is extremely disagreeable.

Cooking is still done on the floor although stand-up counters for stoves were provided.

Windows, such as these at right, are sometimes papered over to assure privacy in the house.

Originally the residential sectors were zoned for one-family-per-house occupancy, but by the admission of the planners themselves, this limit has never been adhered to. Here, again, the causes of different usage are not simple, but the sense of privacy certainly plays a major role in the fact that houses designed for one family are now occupied by three or four.

The Westerner's first response to this apparent crowding is to attribute it to economic necessity: the original tenant rents out part of his house because he needs the money. Yet Chandigarh, by Indian standards, is a wealthy city where people live relatively comfortably, and the houses that are sublet are not the smaller ones, but larger, middle-class houses. Although, to a degree, economics may be a factor, it cannot be the entire answer. In our own culture we so value our privacy and our status as single-family house dwellers that we would share our home only as a last economic resort. "Taking in a lodger" is a sign of hard times, not a middle-class way of life. However, I believe it is so prevalent in Chandigarh primarily because Indians have traditionally lived in extended families in close physical quarters. Their concept of individual privacy differs from ours and can be maintained in closer contact with other people.

These large, extended-family houses in Delhi focus on the inside family life. The exterior attributes of an expensive single-family house in this country—such as the lawn and fence—are not important to the Indians.

Ambiance

The vindication of the modern ideology must be in its giving something that is recognizably "better." But that does not mean only closed sewers and indoor plumbing; it means improving or at least maintaining the quality of life—that elusive element made up of many intangibles that, in sum, add up to human dignity. The single most telling failure of Chandigarh is its lack of "Indianness." Its spaces are too open, its roads too broad. The traditionally dense Indian city is sliced up into thirty separate islands, each too sparsely populated to have an urban atmosphere. The closeness and human contact that characterize Indian life cannot survive in this city as it was planned, and there is no way the transplant can take root. We were told by a long-time resident: "Hygienically we are advanced. Socially we are backward."

Pedestrian's Paradise in Sector 17 of Chandigarh.

Commercial street in downtown Amritsar in the Punjab.

SANAA, YEMEN

Yemen was untouched by the modern Western world before the 1962 revolution that overthrew the absolute government of the Imam. During centuries of seclusion from the West, the whole country, and particularly its capital, Sanaa, evolved a uniquely practical and sophisticated urban architecture. In the decade following the revolution, these traditions were nearly obliterated.

Immediately following the overthrow, the Egyptians occupied the country and remained there until the 1967 Arab-Israeli War forced them to pull out. Since then the Yemeni have been the recipients of aid in the form of foreign building experts from many countries, both Eastern and Western. Regardless of where they came from, the experts had one thing in common. Having been educated in modern building methods, they thought only in modern terms and failed entirely to see the city's architectural wealth. They did not question the appropriateness of their methods because they assumed that eventually the local people would abandon their traditions and adopt the modern architectural approach. Inevitably they complained about the problems of building in the nether world, of local difficulties in mastering modern techniques, of delays in getting the proper materials and, not least, of the difficulties in matching modern materials and methods to the local skills.

The foreign builders in Yemen have had considerable agonies in these several respects, but applying modern building techniques posed seri-

New concrete buildings on Abdul Moghni Street in Sanaa, Yemen.

ous problems for the host country as well. The modern techniques demanded skills and materials that were not available locally. When the decision was made to use modern materials such as reinforced concrete, it meant that the majority of better jobs and higher wages necessarily went to the people outside the country, and also that most of the construction money left the country. Approximately 90 percent of the building cost went for foreign-produced materials. The expense of imported skills and materials forced the cost of construction up four times what it would have been had traditional techniques been used.

All of these problems might have been tolerable if the final product had been better than what was already there, but it was not.

The foreign experts all built in reinforced concrete. In Sanaa there can be a temperature differential of 30 to 40 degrees Fahrenheit in twenty-four hours. Expansion due to temperature changes causes problems even in our moderate climate, but in Sanaa the temperature problem was aggravated because it was difficult to insure that the sand and water used in mixing the concrete were absolutely free from foreign matter. Used to their traditional masonry construcion techniques that allowed for greater error, the local builders found it difficult, and unnecessary from their point of view, to conform to the more stringent requirements of building. As a result, expansion cracks developed in all of these newly built structures within months of completion. These were often not mere cosmetic problems, but endangered the structure of the building.

Expansion cracks in recent concrete construction.

The traditional materials, on the other hand, have few problems with regard to temperature change. As an example of the general durability of Yemeni construction: When the Yemeni Jews moved out of the Jewish Quarter of Sanaa in 1948, the other Yemenis expected them to return, and for nearly ten years the houses in that quarter were unoccupied. When it was clear that they would not come back, the Yemenis began moving in. After ten years of neglect most of the houses needed only a new coat of mud plaster on the roof. The job requires no exceptional skill. You can do it yourself, or if you do not have time, skilled people are readily available. Materials are not a problem either; the earth comes from the backyard, the water from the well.

The modern buildings suffered from another problem too: as the temperature changed outside, it also changed inside. The buildings became ovens in the day and refrigerators at night. In a short time the wealthy Yemenis, who had wanted the status of a modern house, moved back into their traditionally built houses and rented the modern ones to visiting foreigners.

The temperature problems could have been solved by heating and air conditioning, but the high cost of the units and fuel and maintenance are obvious. Furthermore, our concept of climate control was foreign to the Yemeni, who had been using a much more sophisticated method since the time of the Queen of Sheba. The method is still used, but the foreign experts never considered it.

Traditional Yemeni stone construction in Sanaa. The lunette over the window will receive a decorative plaster screen inset with stained glass.

New house with traditional construction in Sanaa, Yemen.

New house with modern construction in Sanaa, Yemen.

The walls of a traditional Yemeni house are thick, usually eighteen inches. One- or two-story houses are usually made of mud bricks, whereas taller ones (up to eight floors in Sanaa) have their foundations and first stories made of stone and the upper ones of fired brick. There are three types of windows in the Yemeni house. The first, which is ornamental, consists of one or two carved plaster screens inset with stained glass and is placed above the second type, a normal casement window. The third type is a small hole—as small as 4" x 12"—with a door; several of these may be put in each room at high and low points on the walls, and opening and closing them controls the air circulation. The combination of structure and ventilation is efficient.

Seven- and eight-story houses are built in Sanaa. Stone is used for the lower floors and baked brick for the upper ones.

In a test made in a one story mud-brick home, the inside temperature varied by only two degrees Fahrenheit over a twenty-four-hour period while the exterior temperature changed by thirty degrees. The interior remained around 69 degrees Fahrenheit.

Most important, Sanaa is not an architectural museum. Its extraordinary architecture is being added to daily. The skills that built it are not gone, though they were nearly lost due to the insistence on being modern that dominated the country for nearly a decade. Fortunately for Yemen, its architectural traditions are now in less danger of being destroyed because of the work of a United Nations' planner named Alain Bertaud. During the three years—1970 to 1973—that Bertaud worked in Yemen he reacquainted the Yemenis with the technical and aesthetic values of their own architecture.

Small ventilation windows are located between the larger window sets in the traditional Yemeni house.

The most successful tactic he used was to build his own home using mud brick in the traditional Yemeni style. The fact that Bertaud and his family would live in a local house, and that other foreigners came and approved of it, was a revelation to the Yemenis. For the first time a foreigner who had come to tell them how to live had told them that they were doing fine by themselves. The psychological impact of this unusual occurrence cannot be overestimated. Soon members of government and other influential Yemenis were admitting that they had never really liked the foreign houses. They had been made to feel ashamed of their own and had been afraid to risk the foreigners' ridicule by choosing their old ways over new ones.

The tentative but encouraging renaissance of Yemeni architecture now underway gives an unusual glimpse into an undermining process that normally goes unnoticed until it is too late. When the experts came to Yemen, the country offered them a remarkable gift of practical and inexpensive local materials and the skilled craftsmen who could use them artfully. Yet the sensitive, knowledgeable professionals failed to take advantage of this rare natural resource. The slight may be partly explained by the persistent Western myth that holds technology to be synonymous with progress; it has mesmerized us to the point where we routinely consider only those solutions familiar to us rather than ask frankly whether the local solutions are not better than what we offer. It is as a result of this state of mind that the indigenous architecture of many countries has never seriously been considered as a workable solution to existing housing needs and has been reduced to an archeological curiosity.

Another effect of the foreign experts' arrogance is more tragic, for by ignoring the sophisticated living architecture of Sanaa they condemned it in the eyes of the Yemenis. We have always been comforted when the materially less fortunate people of the world have envied our technological achievements and material wealth. The novelty of our gadgets is enchanting and often seduces the uninitiated into believing their old ways are hopelessly backward. We, in turn, are tricked, mistaking the awe for a sign of approval, and using it as proof that we are right in our natural tendency to impose our way of doing things. In admiring our miraculous accomplishments, the Yemenis lost sight of the fact that the architectural imports were both expensive and unnecessary.

Increasingly now, there are signs of rebellion. West Germany gave Sanaa a modern, fully-equipped airport in 1973, but when the Yemenis discovered that the airport was to *look* modern as well as be fitted with modern equipment, the government objected. Since the Germans refused to build the airport in the Yemeni style, as soon as it was finished, the government proudly had the glass and steel building wrapped in traditional Yemeni stonework, complete with decorative motifs.

Bertaud's Yemeni-style house proved to be a turning point in the Yemenis' rediscovery of their traditional architecture.

V.

Conclusion

THE PERSISTENCE OF MODERNISM

In spite of periodically reiterated protestations, the tenets of modernism persist. Architects continue to pursue nineteenth-century ideals, guided by nineteenth-century principles. The same messianic state of mind persists, promoted by architects arguing from fundamentally the same set of a priori, pseudo-ethical principles. Most architects continue to impose their own ideals of beauty and social truth and seldom admit the possibility that their may not be the only way. Thirty years ago, in her book *The Chrysanthemum and The Sword*, the social anthropologist Ruth Benedict pinpointed the problem with her analysis of traditional Japanese culture:

> [The] protagonists of One World have staked their hopes on convincing people of every corner of the earth that all the differences between East and West, black and white, Christian and Mohammedan, are superficial and that all mankind is really like-minded.... It sometimes seems as if the tender-minded could not base a doctrine of good will upon anything less than a world of peoples, each of which is a print from the same negative. But to demand such uniformity as a condition of respecting another nation is as neurotic as to demand it of one's wife or one's children. The tough-minded are content that differences should exist....[30]

AVAILABLE TOOLS: BEHAVIORAL INFORMATION

The problem is not that architects have no way to get reliable information about other people's values. Techniques for finding form-relevant social information do exist and are continually being refined, but most architects resist their application. Using such criteria appears to undermine the architect's authority on a front that has heretofore been secure—knowing how people want to live. The problem is further complicated by the kind of vanity that urges us to believe that most people share our values and would like to live the way we do if they were only given the chance.

We make rationalizations to reinforce these feelings. Behavioral data are vague, we argue, particularly when compared to the engineer's calculations. Engineering has an aura of pure science about it, dealing as it does with measurable quantities such as compression stress per square inch. Behavioral data, on the other hand, are imprecise: the need to "feel" a connection to the street is unquantifiable. Even the qualities of the connection can be ambiguous. Data on behavioral science will never be as precise as other types of information, such as the strength of materials, for example, because social relations are obviously infinitely more complex than the subjects of other sciences. It may in fact be dangerous to try to get "scientifically accurate" behavioral data, but even now behaviorists can provide information and insights that are at least comparable in sophistication to the calculations that enabled engineers to build the first great bridges and towers.

THE ARCHITECT'S PREDICAMENT

A Question of Style

Once it has been decided to accommodate behavioral differences, the question is what should the building look like—and how do we establish the criteria for making these visual choices? Modernists' decisions about appearance were based on pseudo-ethical criteria and poetic associations with technology. But the appearance of a building has too far-reaching an impact for it to be determined by homilies.

Old buildings and cities are valuable repositories of a visual heritage, evoking associations that are significant parts of our lives as individuals and as a society. Their contribution is too vital to ignore.

A well-known designer recently visiting the modern quarter of Bagnols sur Cèze, a medieval French town, was photographing the modern buildings when a butcher came out of his shop and stopped her. "Why do you take pictures here?" he asked. "Let me show you the beautiful part of the city." He left his store and took her two blocks away to the old town. "This," he said with pride, "is where I take my family for pleasure on Sundays."

Bagnols sur Cèze: The new (left) and the old (right). (Photo by Eva Zeisel)

Many beautiful traditional cities still exist that need not be sacrificed to modernism. It is a mistake to assume automatically that old cities must be sacrificed to meet modern requirements. Often relatively minor changes, such as the addition of a modern sewage system, are all that is needed. The appearance of buildings need not be "updated."

Some of the houses in Sanaa, Yemen, are centuries old. Others have been built or added to within the past year.

Originality

If the guide lines for the building's appearance are to be set more strictly by its visual context or the social value of its iconography, our understanding of "originality" must change. Originality, or creativity, has become synonymous with "new" and "different," and designing to fit in rather than to stand out seems a terrifying sacrifice of the designer's ego. It is not. It only represents a change in the ground rules: the prevailing aesthetic of the place is substituted for the architect's aesthetic. Instead of being guided by his own narrowly defined "modern" ideas of what is visually pleasing, the architect substitutes another, probably equally narrow set of visual guidelines; he designs to fit in with the existing visual context or to respect the preferences of the clients who are to use the building.

This does not mean that architects should necessarily produce facsimiles of historical relics, although the average traditional building in a traditional context often looks better than an average modern building in the same traditional context. Some modern buildings do fit in with their surroundings without sacrificing their modernity. The Yale dormitories of Eero Saarinen are reasonably successful in capturing the feeling of their academic gothic neighbors without copying them. The Torre Valasca in Milan shows that even a modern building of different scale than its surroundings can grace a traditional cityscape. Other less well publicized examples are all around us, but unfortunately these are exceptions. Only occasionally does a modern building accept the fact of its context rather than try to shock by its modernity.

The modern house sits uncomfortably next to the more traditionally styled one in the photo at the top. (Neighbors finally forced the owner of the former to tear it down.) In the lower photo, the houses on the left are modern versions, complete with garages, of the eighteenth-century town houses facing them in the background. Both modern and traditional-modern houses are in Alexandria, Virginia.

Saarinen's Stiles and Morse Colleges at Yale University recall the academic Gothic of their neighbors, in the background, without actually copying them. (1962)

The Torre Valasca in Milan, shown here at a distance and closer up, takes its silhouette from such medieval predecessors as Florence's the Palazzo Vecchio in the third photograph. Torre Valasca; Belgiojoso, Peressutti, Rogers; 1958.

Originally built in the eighteen-seventies this group of New York City houses was remodeled in 1916 by Harvey Wiley Corbett so that the buildings retained their individuality rather than being standardized into one large uniform block.

A sensitive renovation along the Grand Canal in Venice. Regulatory plans in many older cities are successful in retaining a visually coherent cityscape.

A cultural symbol becomes a commercial symbol. The Acapulco Princess Hotel; William Rudolph Associates, Architects; 1971.

The room on the left with the large "fan" window was added in 1967 to the 1782 Georgian house in Alexandria, Virginia. Architect, David R. Rosenthal.

Elements of the traditional Jamaican Georgian architecture seen left were combined with a modern plan in the private house below. Private house in Silver Sands, Jamaica; Brent C. Brolin, architect; 1969.

This house, shown first by itself above and then in its suburban context below, was designed for John D. Prete to fit into its development context in Woodbridge, Connecticut. Peter Millard, architect; 1973.

The Goffe Street Fire Station in New Haven, Connecticut, designed by Robert Venturi in 1975, fits in well with the neighboring commercial buildings, such as the one shown below, because it uses the same basic vocabulary of shapes and materials, though in a more sophisticated way.

The Architect's Sphere of Influence

Architects usually place the blame for lack of popular acceptance of the modern style on public ignorance of beauty, functional requirements or the spirit of the times; they do not see that it is more a matter of the architect's own failure to recognize that his ideals have seldom coincided with the accepted symbols and values of the public.

It is easy to be righteously indignant and to claim that the general public's disinterest in or dissatisfaction with modern architecture is due to the poor taste of the middle classes. If we look down our noses at people, we can avoid the disturbing thought that they have aesthetic and social preferences that deserve as much consideration as those of the modern architecture buff who wants something dazzlingly different for his Long Island beach house. The elite may be condescending in this way, but this is not an entirely appropriate tack for architects to take.

Painters can challenge the mind and eye if they choose, but they do not, at the same time, automatically impose their own vision of the world on others. Their paintings are hung in a gallery or home, and people can look or not, as they please. The architect is in a different position since people often have little choice about where they work, where they live or what they see in the streets through which they pass.

There are few things the architect can actually affect through his craft. He cannot produce visual order by making an instant and appropriate style for the times, and he cannot change family structure by fixing walls within the home or by making them flexible. The fifty-year-old attempt to educate through architecture has failed. We must relinquish the belief that people are morally elevated by virtue of sharing our aesthetic values.

The architect has relatively clear control over only two areas:

1. Whether the building fits in harmoniously with its surroundings or conflicts with them, and

2. Whether the building conflicts with or accommodates the way of life of the people who must use it.

Until recently, newly industrializing countries have tended to embrace Western culture as a sign of progress and grasped at almost anything Western with a hunger that we took as obvious proof of our cultural superiority. The familiar, traditional ways of life looked pale in comparison with what seemed promised by the immense material wealth and technological skills of the West.

Often the first few generations in America have shed what they could of the past, whereas the following generations, sensing the loss, try to piece together the skills and customs of their past from the partial knowledge that remains.

When I returned from Yemen, I met a third-generation Yemeni who was fascinated with the photos and objects that I had brought back. With visible emotion he told me how strongly he wanted to know about his past, to have a feeling of the place his parents had left. Yet when he tried to arrange for me to show my slides to the local Yemeni community in Brooklyn, he could arouse no interst from the older generation. They wanted no part of their past, while their children searched desperately for it.

There are certainly important reasons for people in traditional societies to desire change—such as better medical care and increased food-producing capability. And, surely, with these important improvements will come other changes. But if traditional physical contexts must change to some degree because of essential modernization, the new physical arrangements should be as well adapted as possible to the traditional living patterns that they will continue to accommodate.

The Past

Desite what the prophets of change say, traditions do persist. The very processes of industrialization are modulated by pre-industrial social mechanisms.

Many observers, including Karl Marx, assumed that India would have to destroy the caste system before it could move into the modern world, but in their book *The Modernity of Tradition*, Professors Lloyd and Susanne Rudolph note that although three hundred and fifty years of British rule failed to eliminate the caste system, India, nevertheless, moved into the industrial age. In fact, they contend, the caste structure actually helped the process by dividing Indian society into well-defined groups with common backgrounds and interests that were to be useful as relatively easy-to-mobilize interest groups. These caste-related groups, in turn, have been able to bring about reforms, including, in some cases, the alleviation of caste oppression.

Because of its phenomenal industrial growth since the war, Japan is often described as being one of the most "Westernized" countries, by which we imply the acceptance of our values. Yet, in a sense, Japan's successful reentrance into the modern world was facilitated by the persistence of a thoroughly Japanese tradition that continues to distinguish its industry. Obedience and teamwork, traits that characterize the modern Japanese worker, can be traced back to the days of feudalism, when the Japanese lord protected his subjects in return for their complete loyalty. Today the corporation is simply substituted for the feudal lord as the object of the worker's obedience.

Modern architects have intentionally ignored the importance of the fact that the present and future are rooted in the past. Throughout history traditions have been modified to fit new situations while retaining much of their original social purpose. The question has only been how easily the new situation could be accommodated by the traditional framework.

Emperor Constantine made a great break with the past when, in 313 A.D., he officially decreed that the Christian God was to be worshipped in place of the old Roman gods, but the shift was made easier by Christianizing secondary Roman gods. The Classical Winged Victory became the Christian angel, and other lower-echelon gods were replaced by Christian saints.

When South Pacific headhunters were forbidden to capture and display their neighbors' heads on their walls, they began taking their outboard motors instead. Now these hang on the walls and afford the same social standing that the heads gave before.

We in the West, particularly in the United States, find it difficult to understand the importance of tradition. We look to the future for the good life, partly because we worship progress in the form of science and technology, which, we seem to feel, can solve all problems. Change has become our tradition—we hesitate not to change for fear of falling behind—and we find it difficult to conceive of the value of continuity. But as long as continuity does not imply rigidity, it is a powerful and positive force.

The changes that we can observe in traditional cultures now industrializing are not that far-reaching and have less to do with architecture than we had imagined. For example, the sense of privacy that governs one's perception of architectural space has seldom been shown to change, and this is precisely the realm in which the architect works. He can only accommodate or disrupt.

It is crucial that traditional ways of life be given the chance to continue and that visual heritages not be lost. One third of the world's population faces the strains of adapting to the impositions of industrial culture, but industrialization does not mean that familiar customs and cultural symbols must automatically be abandoned. Some aspects of traditional cultures can and probably should be reinforced within their new industrialized context.

THE FUTURE

Hopefully, as the value of tradition is rediscovered, we will not just formulate another set of preconceived ideas—this time about the proper way to make a building fit in or the proper way to accommodate behavioral patterns. Such a development would be almost as harmful as to ignore these two important questions entirely.

Instead of another ideology we need something subtler and more flexible: another state of mind. We need to acknowledge, without fear of losing our individuality, that values other than the architect's deserve first consideration. This does not mean that these social values are the only ones to be considered, only that respecting the dignity of the client at least demands their accommodation. Beyond that the architect can offer his own alternatives. It is always when he has offered *only* his own alternatives that he has invited disaster.

This new state of mind does not require that architects suppress their creativity. The bounds of creativity can be broadened in the refined exploration of the craft of architecture, encompassing such problems as how skillfully the designer can evoke the spirit of a place (whether it be modern or traditional) through mass, detail, texture and the other tools of his visual craft. By using what exists as a stepping stone for what is to come, the architect can reinforce rather than undermine the character of neighborhoods and cities every time a building is added. If each new building retains something of the old at the same time that it brings something new, the desirable character of a specific place need not be lost.

The extensive "pre-modern" cityscape that still remains is not historical refuse, to be tolerated until it can be bulldozed and replaced by something modern. It is an asset that should be used as a bridge to the future.

Source Notes

1. John Stuart Mill. *Utilitarianism* (1863, original edition). In *The Utilitarians*. Dolphin Books. New York: Doubleday & Co., Inc., 1961, pp. 406–7.

2. Adolph Loos. *Ornament and Crime*. Quoted in Reyner Banham's *Theory and Design in the First Machine Age*, Second Edition. New York: Praeger Pubs., 1960, p. 94.

3. Sant' Elia. Excerpt from a *Messaggio* as it appeared in the exhibition catalogue of the Nuove Tendenze, May 1914. Quoted in Banham. See note 2, p. 129.

4. Charles Gwathmey is the architect quoted. *The New York Times Magazine*. January 21, 1973.

5. Bronislaw Malinowski. *Argonauts of the Western Pacific*. New York: E.P. Dutton & Co., 1922, pp. 58–59.

6. Luigi Barzini. *The Italians*. New York: Bantam Books, Inc., 1972, p. 95.

7. Nikolaus Pevsner. *The Sources of Modern Architecture and Design*. New York: Praeger, Pubs., 1968, p. 23.

8. Le Corbusier. *Aircraft*. London: Studio Publications, 1935, caption, Plate 2.

9. Le Corbusier. *Towards a New Architecture*. New York: Praeger, Pubs., 1970, p. 223.

10. Le Corbusier. *Précisions sur un état présent de l'architecture et de l'urbanisme*. Paris: G. Crès et Cie, 1930, p. 64. Quote translated by author.

11. Le Corbusier. See note 9, p. 17.

12. Herman Muthesius, "Die moderne Bewegung." In *das goldene Buch der Kunst*. W. Spemann, 1901, pp. 1065-66. Translation by Eva Zeisel.

13. J. K. Huysmans. *A Rebours*. Translated by Robert Baldick. Penguin Books, Inc., 1959, pp. 36–37.

14. Herbert Spencer, *First Principles*, Fourth Edition. New York: D. Appleton, 1883, p. 378.

15. Both quotes in the paragraph from Walter Gropius. *The New Architecture and the Bauhaus*. London: Faber & Faber, Ltd., 1935, p. 82.

16. Le Corbusier. See note 9, p. 201.

17. Quoted in *Art et Décoration*. Vol. 47, 1925, p. 132.

18. Le Corbusier. See note 9, p. 210.

19. Sant' Elia. Quoted in Banham. See note 2, p. 128.

20. Le Corbusier. See note 9, p. 9.

21. Walter Gropius. See note 15, p. 20.

22. Ebenezer Howard. *Garden Cities of Tomorrow*, Second Edition. London: S. Sonnenschein & Co., 1902, Introduction.

23. Walter Gropius. "Sociological Premises for the Minimum Dwelling of Urban Industrial Populations." In *Scope of Total Architecture*. Collier Books. New York: The MacMillan Publishing Co., Inc., 1970, p. 98. (Essay originally published 1929.)

24. Alison and Peter Smithson. *Urban Structuring*. New York: Reinhold/Studio Vista, 1967, p. 18.

25. Alison and Peter Smithson. "Scatter" in *Architecture Design*. April 1959, p. 150.

26. Alison and Peter Smithson, eds. *Team 10 Primer*. Cambridge, Mass.: M.I.T. Press, paperback, 1974, p. 52.

27. Alison and Peter Smithson. See note 24, p. 33.

28. "Collective Housing in Africa." In *Architectural Design*. January 1955, p. 150.

29. Walter Gropius. "Organic Neighborhood Planning." In *Scope of Total Architecture*. See note 23, p. 116.

30. Ruth Benedict. *The Chrysanthemum and the Sword*. Boston: Houghton Mifflin Co., 1946, p. 14.

Bibliography

BOOKS

Banham, R. 1969. *The Architecture of the Well-Tempered Environment.* London: The Architectural Press.

———. 1960. *Theory and Design in the First Machine Age.* 2d ed. New York: Praeger Pubs.

Burn, R. S. 1853. *Mechanics and Mechanism.*

Chase, S. 1929. *Men and Machines.* New York: The Macmillan Co.

Crane, W. 1898. *Bases of Design.* London: Geo. Bell & Sons.

———. 1921. *Line and Form.* From lectures given at Manchester School of Art. London: Geo. Bell & Sons.

de Wolfe, I. 1966. *Italian Townscape.* New York: George Braziller, Inc.

de Zurko, E. 1957. *The Origins of Functionalist Theory.* New York: Columbia Univ. Press.

Dresser, C. 1882. *Principles of Decorative Design.*

Garvey, M. A. (of the Middle Temple). 1852. The Silent Revolution: or the Future Effects of Steam and Electricity upon Mankind. London: W. & F. G. Cash.

Gibson, C. R. 1910. *Romance of Modern Manufacture.* Philadelphia: J. B. Lippincott Co.

Giedion, S. 1955. *Mechanization Takes Command.* 2d ed. New York: Oxford Univ. Press, Inc.

———. 1959. *Space, Time and Architecture.* 3rd ed. Cambridge, Mass.: Harvard Univ. Press.

Great Exhibition of 1851. 1851. Official catalog. London: W. Clowes & Sons.

Greenough, G. 1947. *Form and Function.* Berkeley: University of California Press.

Gropius, W. 1965. *The New Architecture and the Bauhaus.* Cambridge, Mass.: M.I.T. Press.

———. 1970. *Scope of Total Architecture.* 4th printing. Collier Books. New York: The Macmillan Co.

Hogarth, W. 1753. *The Analysis of Beauty.*

Howard, E. 1902. Garden Cities of Tomorrow. 2d ed. London: S. Sonnenschein & Co.

Ivins, W. M., Jr. 1964. *Art and Geometry.* New York: Dover Pubns., Inc.

Klingender, F. D. 1970. Art and the Industrial Revolution. Edited and revised by A. Elton. New York: Schocken Books, Inc.

Laslett, P. 1965. *The World We Have Lost: England Before the Industrial Age.* New York: Charles Scribner's Sons.

Le Corbusier. 1935. *Aircraft.* London: Studio Publications.

———. 1926. *L'art décoratif d'aujourd'hui.* Paris: G. Crès et Cie.

———. 1971. *The City of Tomorrow.* Trans. by Frederick Etchells.

Cambridge, Mass.: M.I.T. Press.

———. 1930. *Precision sur un etat present de l'architecture et de l'urbanisme.* Paris: G. Cres et Cie.

———. 1970. *Towards a New Architecture.* New York: Praeger, Pubs.

Morris, W. 1901. *Art and Its Producers, and the Arts and Crafts of Today.* Two addresses delivered before the National Association for the Advancement of Art.

———. 1968. *Selected Writings and Designs.* Edited by A. Briggs. Gloucester, Mass.: Peter Smith, Publisher.

National Electric Light Association. Ca. 1928. *The Romance of Power.*

Nicholson, J. 1853. *Operative Mechanic.* 4th ed.

Osborne, H. 1970. *Aesthetics and Art Theory: an Historical Introduction.* New York: Dutton paperback.

Ozenfant, A. 1952. *Foundations of Modern Art.* Augmented American ed. New York: Dover Pubns.

Pevsner, N. 1968. *The Sources of Modern Architecture and Design.* New York: Praeger, Pubs.

Polanyi, K. 1968. *Primitive, Archaic and Modern Economies.* Edited by G. Dalton. Anchor paperback ed. New York: Doubleday & Co., Inc.

Pugin, A. W. 1841. *Contrasts.* London: C. Dolman.

———. 1841. *The True Principles of Pointed or Christian Architecture.* London: J. Weale.

Pye, D. 1964. *The Nature of Design.* Reinhold Pub. Corp.

Redgrave, R. 1851. Exhibition of 1851, London. *Supplementary Report on Design.*

———. 1853. *On the Necessity of Principles in Teaching Design.* London: Chapman & Hall.

Rudolph, Lloyd and Susanne. 1967. *The Modernity of Tradition.* Univ. of Chicago Press.

Ruskin, J. 1961 (1848, orig. pub. date). *The Seven Lamps of Architecture.* New York: The Noonday Press.

Sitte, C. 1965. (1889, orig. pub. date). *City Planning According to Artistic Principles.* Trans. by G. R. Collins and C. C. Collins. London: Phaidon Press, Ltd.

Smithson, Alison and Peter. 1967. *Urban Structuring.* Edited by J. Lewis. New York: Reinhold/Studio Vista.

van de Velde, H. 1929. *Le nouveau, son apport à l'architecture et aux industries d'art.* Edited by les Amis de l'Institut Supérieur des Arts Decoratifs, Brussels.

Weber, M. 1958. *The Protestant Ethic and the Spirit of Capitalism.* New York: Charles Scribner paperback.

Whewell, W. 1854. *The World of Science, Art and Industry: New York Exhibition of 1853–54.* Edited by Silliman, Goodrich et al. New York: G. P. Putnam's, Sons.

——. 1852. *Lectures on the Results of the Great Exhibition Delivered Before the Society of Arts, Manufacturers and Commerce.* London: David Bogue.

PERIODICALS AND REPORTS

Aahren, U. "Contemporary Architecture Compared with Architecture of the Past: From the Social Point of View," Report of 15th International Congress of Architects at Washington, D.C., September 24–30, 1939.

"Architecture of the Middle East." Special issue, *Architectural Design*, 27 (March 1957).

Banham, R. "Criticism: Park Hill Housing, Sheffield." *Architectural Review*, December 1961, pp. 402–410.

——. "What Architecture of Technology?" *Architectural Review*, 131 (1962).

Barry, E. M. "Architecture and Utility." *American Architect*, 7 (1880): 92.

Becket, E. "On the Frailties of Architects." *American Architect*, 3, no. 118 (1878).

Booraem, H. T. "Architectural Expression in a New Material." *Architectural Record*, April 1908, pp. 249–68.

Boudon, P. "Pessac." *Archiectural Design*, September 1969.

Boyington, W. W. "Architecture at the Present Time As Compared with That of Fifth Years Ago." *American Architect*, 22 (1887): 205.

Brolin, B. and Zeisel, J. "Mass Housing: Social Research and Design." *Architectural Forum*, July/August 1968, pp. 66–71.

Brolin, B. "Chandigarh was planned by experts, but something has gone wrong." *Smithsonian*, 1972, pp. 56–63.

"CIAM 10 Projects." *Architectural Design*. 25 (September 1955).

Crane, W. "The English Revival of the Decorative Arts." *Fortnightly Review*, December 1892, pp. 810–22.

Dickens, C. "Architectural Doers and Talkers." *All the Year Round*, 1870.

Drake and Lasdun. "Cluster Blocks at Bethnal Green." *Architectural Design*, 27 (February 1958): 62–64.

Drew, J. "Chandigarh Capital City Project." Edited by Trevor Dannatt. *Architect's Yearbook*, pub. by Elek Bks. Ltd., 5 (1953).

Greenough, H. "American Architecture." *Southern Literary Messenger*, 19 (1853) 513.

"Heroic Period of Modern Architecture." Special issue, *Architectural Design*, December 1965.

International Exposition of Modern Decorative & Industrial Arts in Paris, 1925. Report of Commission appointed by U.S. Secretary of Commerce.

Loos, A. "Ornament et crime." *L'Espirit nouveau*, 2 (November 1920): 159–168.

Marinetti, F. T. "Futurist Manifesto." *L'Esprit nouveau*, 3 (December 1920): 303–305.

Maus, O. "Les industries d'art au salon de la libre esthetique." *Art et decoration*, I (1897): 44–48.

Moser, J., F.A.I.A. "The Search for an American Style." *American Architecture*, 21(1887): 16.

Nairn, I. "Spec-Built: 1. The Four Failures. 2. A Few Successes." *Architectural Review*, March 1961, pp. 163–81.

Pahl, R. E. "Is the Mobile Society a Myth?" *Architectural Design*. September 1968, pp. 412–15.

Potter, W. A. "Some Failures in American Architecture." *American Architecture*, 7 (1880): 27.

Smithson, Allison and Peter. "Aesthetics of Change." *Architects Yearbook*, 8 (1957): 14.

——. "An Alternative to the Garden City Idea." *Architectural Design*, 26 (July 1956): 229.

——. "Cluster City." *Architectural Review*. November 1957, pp. 333–36.

——. "Criteria for Mass Housing." *Architectural Design*. September 1967, pp. 393–94.

——. "Scatter." *Architectural Design*, April 1959, p. 149.

——. "The Function of Architecture in Cultures-in-Change." *Architectural Design*, April 1960, p. 149.

Taylor, N. "The Failure of Housing." *Architectural Review*, November 1967, pp. 341–59.

"Team 10." Special issue, *Architectural Design*, April 1960.

van de Velde, H. "Raison et fantaisie." 15th International Congress of Architects at Washington, D.C., I, September 24–30, 1939.

Index